SYNAGOGUE ARCHITECTURE IN AMERICA

FAITH, SPIRIT & IDENTITY

SYNAGOGUE ARCHITECTURE IN AMERICA

FAITH, SPIRIT & IDENTITY

Henry & Daniel Stolzman

Tami Hausman, Ph.D., editor
Memo Productions, art direction

images
Publishing

First published in Australia in 2004 by
The Images Publishing Group Pty Ltd
ABN 89 059 734 431
6 Bastow Place, Mulgrave, Victoria, 3170, Australia
Telephone: +61 3 9561 5544 Facsimile: +61 3 9561 4860
Email: books@images.com.au
Website: www.imagespublishinggroup.com

Copyright © The Images Publishing Group Pty Ltd
The Images Publishing Group Reference Number: 412

National Library of Australia
Cataloguing-in-Publication entry:

Stolzman, Henry
Faith, Spirit, and Identity: Synagogue Architecture in America

Bibliography
ISBN: 1 86470 074 2.

1. Synagogues – United States – Design and construction.
2. Architecture, Jewish – United States. 3. Judaism – United States.
I. Stolzman, Daniel. II. Title

726.30973

Coordinating Editor: Robyn Beaver
Production by The Graphic Image Studio Pty Ltd, Melbourne, Australia
Website: www.tgis.com.au
Film by Mission Productions Limited, Hong Kong
Printed by Everbest Printing Co., Ltd. in Hong Kong/China

For Ali and Kas...

who make us whole.

FOREWORD

America has accorded the Jews unparalleled opportunities for economic advancement, social integration, and personal fulfillment. With these uncommon privileges and possibilities, have emerged daunting challenges to the preservation of Jewish faith, identity and commitment within this accepting country. To the extent that the United States has welcomed the Jews, it has also invited and enticed them to forego those beliefs and practices that have long made them and kept them a distinct people.

This basic truism about the more than 350 years of Jewish life in America lies at the heart of this admirable and accessible work. This book explores, through the medium of American synagogue architecture and the sagas of Jewish congregational life, the question of how those Jews who wished to maintain links to their ancestral past expressed their concerns about survival under freedom through the construction of their houses of worship.

The calculus of adherence to past ways and affinity for innovation in synagogue construction—as in community life generally—has varied from period to period and among the several Jewish streams: Orthodoxy, Conservatism, Reform and Reconstructionism. Upon arrival in this country, immigrant Jews—traditional, if not Orthodox, in their manner and bearing—built structures that comported with their recollections of their European pasts and only partially reflected their incipient identities as Americans. As these newcomers grew and advanced in this country, they, and most especially their children, constructed synagogues that spoke of their quests for increased acceptance and respectability even if memories of the Jewish past still loomed large in their collective consciousness. Ultimately, their descendants, our present-day community, so comfortable within this country's polity, but worried that so many Jews are losing touch with all that is Jewish, have looked to their houses of worship to create and to instill meaningful and enduring Jewish allegiances.

Casual readers of the Stolzmans' masterful work will focus on the detailed expositions and illustrations of representative synagogues for each period of American Jewish history. As such, it is a magnificent Jewish art book. More deeply engaged students will appreciate the message of Jewish survival contained in this uncommon book of Jewish history. And all who ponder the implications of this examination of our people's life will be elevated by the thoughtful and uplifting introduction to the spiritual dimensions of synagogue life provided by Professor Lawrence Hoffman.

OPPOSITE: *Contemporary Torah stand, West End Synagogue, New York, New York (1996).*

JEFFREY S. GUROCK
LIBBY M. KLAPERMAN PROFESSOR OF JEWISH HISTORY
YESHIVA UNIVERSITY
OCTOBER 1, 2003

CONTENTS

One Saturday morning last fall, I looked out of my Upper West Side apartment
window and watched various groups of Sabbath observers on the street below.
From either the faces I recognized, or the clothes they wore, or the items they carried,
I knew that they represented a broad array of American Jewry. As they rushed off to
their synagogues, I was reminded anew of the importance of synagogue life in America
and was humbled by the task I had undertaken in writing this book.

The impetus for this study came from my own explorations as an architect
working on synagogue commissions. In meeting with building committees comprised
of both lay members and clergy, I began to understand that we all approached our
building projects with the same goal: to find designs that represented both our Jewish
and American cultures. While the task is easily enough stated, it is more difficult to
achieve. What are appropriate ways for expressing Jewish roots in current buildings?
How do we build buildings that celebrate our Jewish past, serve our contemporary
communal psyche, and announce our futures?

Our desire to avoid repeating past solutions led us to study synagogue history
to see how others through the centuries have accomplished this. How have other
congregations resolved the tensions between being Jewish and American, sacred and
secular, modern and traditional? The fruits of these investigations provided the seeds
for this book.

This book was to be a photographic survey of American synagogues that would
answer those questions. I started with a simple premise: American synagogue
architecture, like architecture of the Jewish Diaspora in general, mirrors local—in this
case American—trends in architecture as it reflects Jewish culture. During the course
of our research, however, my son Daniel and I came to realize that establishing this
point would require an understanding of the history of American synagogues and the
Jews who built them. So the book grew into a historical exploration of the synagogue,
from its inception over two thousand years ago to the present day. Regarding the
specific subject of the book, the American synagogue, we collected a broad sample of
American synagogues which best demonstrated our premise. The following collection
of synagogue buildings expresses, in bricks and mortar, the aspirations of the
congregations that built them.

Photographs, however, are only two-dimensional images. Missing here are the
feelings of the spaces, the sounds of the chanting of Torah, the rustlings of children,
the greetings of congregants, the haunting cadences of prayer. These are the
ingredients that bring our synagogues to life. While we have noted the architects and
scholars who have contributed to American synagogue design, we could not in the
confines of this book honor those who have truly invigorated our synagogues: the
congregants who dedicate their energy and resources to synagogue life. I thank them
for their tireless efforts.

OPPOSITE: *Sanctuary, North
Shore Congregation Israel,
Glencoe, Illinois (1964).*

ABOVE: *Wailing Wall,*
Jerusalem, Israel (2003).

Gratitude must also be expressed to the many people who have assisted us both directly with their time and materials and indirectly with their assistance in producing this document. I am truly indebted to all of them for their input and their patience.

Also to be acknowledged is Douglas Riccardi with whom I have worked on several synagogue projects and who did the superb graphic layouts for the book.

I am particularly grateful to Justin Lubatkin, who energetically scanned the American landscape to find congregations that were to be candidates for inclusion. Justin was there from the outset, enthusiastically encouraging me to undertake this project.

Tami Hausman, an integral part of the tripartite team that produced this book, deserves special recognition. Her extensive editing, multiple rewrites of our text, repeated words of encouragement, and persistent demand that we meet deadlines and stay on track were essential to the making of this book. I am thankful to have her as a colleague and as a friend.

Dr. Jeffrey Gurock deserves special recognition for writing the introduction, by which I feel quite honored. I admire Jeffrey's ability to concisely capture and articulate the book's essential points.

This book would be incomplete without Rabbi Larry Hoffman's provocative essay in which he brilliantly explores the roots of contemporary Jewish spirituality and studies the myriad forms of Jewish religious practice today. Larry's incisive thoughts complement the content of the book and, indeed, have inspired much of it.

And of course there is Daniel, my co-author and son, who took on a Herculean task and succeeded even beyond my fatherly expectations.

FURTHER ACKNOWLEDGMENTS

Daniel and I would also like to extend our gratitude to Mike Berk, whose editorial guidance was invaluable, as well as Jayne Merkel, Rabbi Avi Winokur, and Dana Turken, who each provided insightful criticism. We are indebted to the faithful support of Paul Latham, Alessina Brooks and Robyn Beaver at The Images Publishing Group as well as Nancy Egan, who introduced us to Paul. We are also beholden to America's thriving Jewish historical societies and institutions, including the American Jewish Archives at Hebrew Union College in Cincinnati, The Jewish Museum of Maryland, The American Jewish Historical Society, The Jewish Theological Seminary, and The Jewish Museum in New York. Stuart Rockoff, Director of History at the Goldring/Woldenberg Institute of Southern Jewish Life, deserves special mention. We also appreciate Dr. Richard Vosko, Laura Kruger, Bob Immerman, Laurie Gross, and Roberta Gratz, for lending their expertise. Finally, recognition must be given to the congregations included in this book; each has generously provided us with the rich documentation that has made this project possible.

H.S.
New York, June 2003

1 | FAITH, SPIRIT, AND IDENTITY

American synagogues tell the story of American Jews, a people whose culture and identity have evolved dramatically over the last four centuries, and whose religious buildings have changed as a result. Synagogues are thus a physical testament to the religious and ethnic identity of American Jewry; they are far more than just places where people pray. The chronology of American synagogues documents the waves of immigrant Jews who landed in the United States, established their roots, and forged new ways of life.

Throughout their long and rich existence, Jews have constructed synagogues to serve as the social and religious centers of their communities. The word 'synagogue' itself is derived from the Greek *synagein*, which means 'to bring together,' and reflects the synagogue's age-old importance as a community building. Historically the synagogue is considered to have a three-fold purpose. First, it is a house of worship (*Beit Tefilah*). It is also a *Beit Knesset*, or 'house of assembly.' Lastly, the synagogue is a *Beit Midrash*, or 'house of study.' These three functions are at the heart of what makes a synagogue a synagogue.

Despite the constancy of its functions, the physical form of the synagogue has always varied greatly. While churches donned steeples early on, and mosques have long worn domes, synagogues have never had an iconic shape or style that could identify them as uniquely Jewish buildings. Instead, throughout history, synagogue architecture has followed local styles rather than universal patterns of design. From Egypt to China, synagogue buildings have usually fit in perfectly with their neighborhoods. Only the interior spaces of synagogues, equipped with liturgical elements specific to Jewish religious practice, announce their 'Jewishness.'

OPPOSITE: *Daily chapel, Shearith Israel, New York, New York (1897), which contains elements from the original Mill Street Synagogue, the first synagogue built in America.*

Jews from all over the world have immigrated to America. However, since most American Jews descend from European ancestry, early European synagogues are the primary antecedents for synagogues built in the United States. But as we will see, immigrants rarely imported their traditional synagogue architecture when they crossed the Atlantic. Sometimes they did preserve certain elements like seating layouts and various Jewish symbols, but for the most part the synagogues they built took cues from the styles popular in America at the time of their construction.

This phenomenon parallels the way that Jews have always maintained a complex position of being both within and without the societies in which they have lived. Jews have continually renegotiated their identities with the local cultures in which they settled throughout the Diaspora (the area outside ancient Israel settled by Jews). As Jews migrated from region to region, individual Jewish communities erected buildings wherever they could in order to ensure the continued practice of their faith. They built an incredible diversity of structures, reflecting the vast cultural differences among Jews from around the world. In many ways, these religious buildings testify to Jews' ability to securely adapt and assimilate to indigenous ways of life. They have been the means by which Jews have ensured the continuity of their tradition from generation to generation.

American synagogues, therefore, reflect American Jews' status both as Americans and as Jews. In America, Jews have been able to reevaluate their religion more than Jews in any other time or place in history. With relative freedom came greater opportunities for assimilation and with these came greater tensions between Jewish heritage and American values. American Jews became well-established members of the cities and towns in which they lived, truly integrated into mainstream culture, while facing the challenge of redefining themselves as modern Jews.

This book traces the history of the American synagogue from its origins in the Holy Land to its present-day forms in the United States. The first part of the book documents the changes that have occurred in American synagogue design since the first Jewish house of worship, the Mill Street Synagogue, was built in New Amsterdam in 1730. The second part is a photographic compendium of buildings that illustrate the evolution of American synagogue architecture. This survey presents a cross-section of American buildings that were built as synagogues; we have not included structures that were constructed for other functions and later adapted for religious use. Most of the historic buildings featured are still used by congregations today. Others have been designated as landmarks to mark their significance in the history of American Jewry and the country as whole. Naturally there are thousands of other synagogues that deserve equal notice. Unfortunately, due to space limitations and in some cases inadequate documentation, they could not be included in this publication.

As we will see, congregations often built synagogues that symbolically proclaimed their arrival in America, both as acclimated citizens and as Jews. Jewish immigrants had architectural options in the United States that had not always been available in their homelands, and these newfound freedoms fostered experimentation in the style, layout, and function of their synagogues. In America, Jews also built large, impressive synagogues on unprecedented scales, the buildings' visual flamboyance and bold Jewish imagery referring both to Jews' desire to fit in and their impulse to remain apart.

The specific forms and styles of American synagogues have always been influenced by the prevailing fashions of the time. The majority of Jews arrived in the United States during the nineteenth and early twentieth centuries, at a time when in both Europe and America architecture of a civic, religious, and institutional nature was largely inspired by models from the past. This was the period of revivalism, when styles were 'revived' from the depths of antiquity, in part on the basis of new information available as the result of archeological studies. Certain styles were associated with particular symbolic meanings that were used as a way to construct political and cultural identities. Napoleon used immense Roman forms, for example, to equate the military strength and cultural superiority of France with that of the Roman Empire; Thomas Jefferson advocated Greek Classicism be used for national monuments to associate the young country of America with democratic ideals.

Synagogues have been built in every popular style: Georgian, Classical, Gothic, and Modern, to name but a few. Some congregations allowed major stylistic choices to be made by non-Jewish architects, a fact that suggests a relative comfort with American paradigms. There were other decisive moments, however, when American Jews sought out more authentic styles that could preserve and strengthen their collective Jewish identity.

Although relatively well accepted in American society, Jews have always remained a minority; exotic, Eastern-looking architecture distinguished their otherness in a way that was accepted by Jews and non-Jews alike. In this context, since the middle of the nineteenth century American Jews have popularized a succession of architectural styles that were believed to metaphorically convey the Jewish experience. For example, the Romanesque (or Byzantic) and Moorish styles, with their bold clarity of simple forms and exotic decorative patterns, were considered to be evocative of the Jews' roots in the Middle East. In the late nineteenth and early twentieth centuries these exotic or 'Oriental,' styles became popular for a wide cross-section of American building types, but they were felt to be particularly appropriate for synagogues. And before archaeological investigations of Middle Eastern sites began to reveal the actual architecture of biblical buildings, these styles were even thought to have historic precedents in earlier periods of Jewish history—dating as far back as ancient Israel—and were seen as logical references to Jewish tradition.

In the twentieth century, modern architects used bold, abstract forms and sometimes evoked early synagogue models—such as the wooden synagogues of Poland—in their designs. These explorations expressed a quest for authentically Jewish forms that did not blindly copy historical styles of earlier generations. Today, American synagogue design continues to be fertile ground for Jews' ongoing search for identity.

Synagogue building in America has mirrored patterns of Jewish immigration for almost 400 years. Jewish immigration to America is often described as a series of waves; the image is a good one. Jews came here in large numbers when unique situations in their European homelands forced them to do so. The first Jewish immigrants to America arrived in New Amsterdam (present-day New York) in 1654. These Jews were among the earliest European settlers on the continent. As traders, they came to the Americas from Holland, where they had settled after escaping the Spanish Inquisition. In 1730, on Mill Street in New Amsterdam, descendents of these Jews built the first synagogue in North America.

These first immigrants were followed by three more waves of Jewish migration to the United States. The so-called German wave, comprising Ashkenazi Jews from Germany and Central Europe, arrived between the 1820s and the 1880s. Next, a huge influx of Eastern European Jews, from which 80 percent of American Jewry can claim descent, arrived between the 1880s and 1920s. Much later, after World War II, many American Jews abandoned urban centers for the suburbs, an event which represents another kind of migratory 'wave,' this one showing how Jews had truly become American in terms of their values and ways of life.

Each successive wave of immigrants struggled to define the precise balance between the practice of Judaism and the larger social context of living in America. When they first landed, immigrants were complete foreigners; those who arrived in the nineteenth and twentieth centuries contrasted starkly with Jews who had been living in the United States for generations. Even before they had the financial means or social acceptance that would enable them to become builders and owners of their own spiritual homes, the new immigrants established synagogues wherever their congregations could find available space. In time, as Jewish communities became larger and more established, congregations built bigger, more prominent buildings. Demonstrating that they had truly arrived in America, congregations erected important edifices as testaments to their social and economic success, and to compete for the attention of assimilated, non-practicing Jews.

BELOW: *Courtyard at Congregation Agudas Achim, Austin, Texas (2001).*

The practice of Judaism has varied greatly in the United States. As more and more Jews settled here and established local congregations, some adapted their religious practices to suit new lives and values. Today, American Judaism is splintered into four distinct affiliations: Reform, Conservative, Orthodox, and Reconstructionist. In addition, Jews are further divided into Sephardim and Ashkenazim, categories that refer to the part of the world from which they or their ancestors emigrated.

These groups' distinctive practices of Judaism impacted the architecture of Jewish houses of worship. The first and most obvious architectural differences have been found in the internal layouts of synagogue sanctuaries. While the difference between an Orthodox and a Reform synagogue is not usually discernable from the outside, their sanctuaries often reveal their specific affiliations. Reform congregations incorporated Christian traditions, such as the music lofts and organs found in nineteenth-century Protestant churches in America. Orthodox congregations retained Jewish traditions that were brought from Europe, such as galleries for women and partitions that keep women and men separate during worship.

Historical changes in synagogues' roles have also affected design. In the Jewish ghettos of the Diaspora, where Jews had little access to mainstream social and civic institutions, synagogues likely acted as community centers, providing a range of comprehensive programs and social services which their congregants could not get elsewhere. Yet the earliest American synagogues were places of prayer and education only. American Jews participated in social functions outside the synagogue, joining or obtaining benefits from fraternal lodges and benevolent societies that offered assistance programs and charity. Later, these functions were brought into the synagogue in an effort to maintain a coherent Jewish community as Jews started to gain acceptance in secular society.

Now, in the early twenty-first century, synagogues have become the focal point for myriad activities pertaining to American Jewish life. A new American typology predominates: the synagogue as the religious <u>and</u> social center of the Jewish community. While synagogues have always served important community roles (as houses of study and assembly), their social function has been dramatically enhanced, particularly in the last 50 years. Today, the typical American synagogue is a full-fledged community center, Hebrew school, and sometimes a private day school. From gift shops to cafés, youth centers to banquet halls, new elements in synagogue design demonstrate the synagogue's augmented role in Jewish life.

Contemporary synagogue architecture has also responded to the shifting religious values of American Jews. Many American Jewish congregations seek a greater sense of intimacy and community in their synagogues than did their ancestors. As a result, efforts have been made to bring worshippers physically closer to the clergy.

Today, synagogue architecture represents a community that has always danced gracefully between two cultures and continues to evolve in a way that reflects the vitality and dynamism of Jewish life in America.

2 | THE SYNAGOGUE IN HISTORY

American synagogues today are enriched by more than two-and-a-half millennia of Jewish history. When the synagogue emerged in ancient Israel, it marked the dawn of a unique kind of religious architecture that ushered in new liturgical practices. Before then, the most sacred place in the Jewish religion was the Temple in Jerusalem. Though a much larger religious site, the temple was a much more exclusive space than the synagogue. Its design permitted worshippers to enter exterior courts surrounding the temple, but not the sanctuary proper, which was used only by Jewish high priests who conducted ritual sacrifice. By contrast, synagogues were built to provide communal spaces for local constituencies and were expressly designed for use by worshippers. Synagogues were the first religious buildings in the Ancient world to serve a congregation rather than a priestly elite.[1]

Before the appearance of synagogues in the ancient world, the First Temple, or Solomon's Temple, had served as the first Jewish house of worship until it was destroyed by the Babylonians during the sixth century B.C.E.[2] While the nature of the First Temple has in recent years been a subject of debate among scholars, far more is known about the Second Temple, which was later built on the same site. The Second Temple was laid out as a series of courtyards, and access to each was increasingly limited. It was also the site of the Holiest of Holies, a small room which the high priest, or *Kohayn Gadol*, entered once a year on Yom Kippur to intercede on behalf of the Jewish people and pray for the absolution of their sins.

In a sense, synagogues were an architecture of exile, a temporary solution for a post-Temple world. After the destruction of the Second Temple in 70 A.C.E., synagogues became the primary Jewish religious structures. Paradoxically, even though synagogues brought Jews together for centuries, they were a constant reminder that

OPPOSITE: *Bimah, Krakow, Poland*

1   Geoffrey Wigoder, *The Story of the Synagogue: A Diaspora Museum Book,* Harper and Row Publishers, San Francisco, 1986, p. 10.
2   B.C.E refers to 'Before the Common Era,' the period designated as B.C. in the Christian calendar.

the original Temples had been lost, and that Jews had been exiled from the Holy Land. But the synagogue continued to serve an important spiritual and community purpose, and as a building type it eventually became a permanent fixture in Jewish life.

Less restricted and more accessible than the Temples, synagogues opened Jewish religious and social practices to the lay public; local clergy members were close to their communities and provided them with legal and liturgical guidance. Since official, ritual sacrifices could take place only in the Temple, Jewish communities developed new daily prayers to represent symbolically the Temple rites that could no longer take place.

Early synagogues were relatively modest architecturally. Jews adopted a floor plan that was commonly used for civic purposes—the Roman basilica plan—and modified it for religious practice in synagogues. This plan featured a long rectangular hall, typically flanked by two side aisles, that was flexible enough to be used as a reception hall, legal court, or meeting place. The basilica plan worked well for synagogues because its open, expansive rooms could accommodate worship as well as community events.

Most early synagogues were undecorated, functional structures with nondescript façades, and most likely they did not dazzle the eye. Their only identifiable Jewish features consisted of menorahs, rams' horns, and other Jewish motifs that are still used in contemporary American synagogues. Certain icons were unique to the Jews, and their placement—or the lack thereof—on a building façade may have indicated the degree of comfort that a Jewish community felt in local society. Jews generally avoided ostentatious designs, particularly in places where Jews were restricted to a subordinate status. It was safer—and in some cases even obligatory—to keep synagogues simple and iconography to a minimum. Today, the use and type of iconography is still frequently debated among designers of contemporary synagogues.

BELOW: *Remains of an ancient synagogue, Kefar Nahum, Israel.*

Jews had lived in Egypt as far back as the sixth century B.C.E., although they did not leave the Holy Land *en masse* until the Second Temple was destroyed nearly 2000 years ago.[3] Like the Jews of antiquity, those who settled throughout the Diaspora were heavily influenced by local building customs, and they often modeled their synagogues after contemporary mosques and churches.

In both Christian and Muslim-ruled regions, it was common for synagogue design to be restricted by various building regulations. These laws mandated, for example, that synagogues could not be taller than neighboring churches or mosques. In response to such restrictions, some prominent Jews built synagogues in their homes and opened them to local Jewish communities that had no other place to pray. Frequently nestled on upper floors of multi-family dwellings, these private synagogues were concealed from building inspectors and vandals, and they offered protected refuges tucked away from the trials and tribulations of daily life.

As they settled in different parts of the world, Jews absorbed the social practices of their new homes and formulated new rituals and traditions. As a result, distinct Jewish subcultures developed, and today, Jews are subdivided into two groups: Sephardim and Ashkenazim.

The term 'Sephardic' derives from the word 'sepharad,' the Biblical term that refers to the country of Spain; later, the word was used to describe the entire Iberian Peninsula. Jews settled in Spain as early as several centuries before the birth of Christ, when Spain was ruled by the Romans. Jews remained there through the rule of the Christian Visigoths, which began in the fifth century C.E., although they were persecuted during this period. After the Muslims conquered the country in 711, Jews enjoyed a period of unprecedented freedom. They prospered, especially during a period properly known as *la convivencia* ('coexistence') between the eighth and fifteenth centuries, when Muslims, Christians, and Jews lived in relative harmony. At the time, Jewish congregations built lavish synagogues that were heavily influenced by Islamic art and architecture. The great synagogue in Toledo (1200), which has since become the Santa Maria la Blanca church, has a relatively modest exterior, but the interior sanctuary is filled with four rows of octagonal piers. It was directly inspired by Islamic architecture, so much so that it looks almost exactly like a contemporary mosque.

After 1492, Sephardic Jews fled the Spanish Inquisition and took refuge wherever they were allowed, either establishing new Jewish communities in the places they settled or joining existing Jewish communities in such places as Morocco, India, and Persia. Today, we refer to Jews from these areas—people who never set foot in Spain—as Sephardim. Sephardic Jews were the first to arrive in New Amsterdam and settle in the American colonies. Later, in the nineteenth century, American Jews would evoke the pre-Inquisition period in Spain when they chose to build their synagogues in the so-called Moorish revival style.

3 There is actually indication that Jews may have lived in Mesopotamia and other areas outside the land of Israel before the sixth century B.C.E. Egypt, however, is one of the first places in the Diaspora where Jews are known to have lived in significant numbers, as in the city of Alexandria.

Most American Jews are Ashkenazi, meaning that they originally immigrated from Northern, Central, and Eastern Europe. The term derives from the name of Noah's great-grandson Ashkenaz. As early as the medieval period and perhaps before, Jews were using this word to refer to the Germanic world. Although the geographic region they called Ashkenaz was located between northeastern France and the Rhine Valley, its Jewish residents were eventually displaced to the north and east by expulsions, pogroms, and the Christian-led crusades, and the term came to refer to Jewish communities across Europe, from France to the Ukraine.

In places where it was allowed by law, Ashkenazic Jews did build freestanding buildings in the centers of their neighborhoods. These synagogues were built in a variety of styles and featured different seating arrangements, which reflected the architectural character of their immediate locales. Among the earliest models were stone synagogues, which date back as far as the eleventh century; many of them are still standing throughout Central and Eastern Europe. These modest, low-rise structures contained the most basic facilities for Jewish worship.

Jews also borrowed styles from Christian churches. In fact, the oldest synagogue in continuous use in Europe, the Altneushul in Prague, built in the late thirteenth century, was designed in the Gothic style. Like Gothic churches of this period, the synagogue has thick walls, a vaulted masonry ceiling, supporting external buttresses, and various annexes for ancillary functions. Its interior organization is based on a 'double-nave' plan that was derived from the chapter houses of medieval mendicant orders. The two naves have groined, vaulted ceilings that rest on two shared central pillars, while a central reading desk is surrounded by an iron cage, featuring pointed arches typical of Gothic design.

BELOW: *Sinagoga de Santa Maria la Blanca, Toledo, Spain (13th century). Its distinctive octagonal piers are typically found in Islamic architecture.*

Between the seventeenth and nineteenth centuries, a truly remarkable building type—the wooden synagogue—developed in the *shtetlach* (Jewish rural villages) of Poland and was widely copied. Although it is thought to have been inspired by contemporary wooden houses of the Polish nobility, the wooden *shtetl* synagogue was perhaps the most original synagogue type ever to emerge in the Diaspora. It developed when, for the first time, Jews were able to join European craft guilds where they learned building skills such as carpentry, joinery, and decoration. Invigorated by their new freedom, Jewish congregations constructed synagogues with pagoda-like, multi-layered roofs that rose to the sky; their interiors were decorated with elaborate liturgical objects carved by Jewish artisans.

By the early nineteenth century, some European Jews were given the opportunity to join secular, mainstream society. In France, Napoleon categorized Jews as a religious group, rather than a race, which allowed them to enter French civil life—and to enjoy the protections of secular regulations and laws for the first time. The civic and social emancipation of Jews followed in various countries throughout Europe, which meant that Jews could build far more prominent synagogues than those of previous generations. In France, Germany, Poland, Italy, and other nations, Jews built synagogues that reflected the architectural styles associated with the burgeoning nationalism of their native countries. Since dubbed the age of 'cathedral synagogues,'

LEFT: *Wooden synagogue, Poland, since destroyed.*
RIGHT: *Exterior, Altneushul, Prague, 15th century. The interior of this synagogue reflects medieval churches of the same period.*

this era produced magnificent synagogues throughout Europe that were on par with Christian churches, giving Jews a sense of civil and religious legitimacy in relation to their Christian neighbors that was heretofore unimaginable. In some cases, regional governments or national rulers welcomed these buildings as a valid replacement of the historic squalor of Jewish quarters, and even encouraged the architectural ambitiousness of local Jewish communities as an incentive to draw Jews into the mainstream of secular national cultures.

Emancipation also brought mobility. As rural Jews left their insular towns, many chose the larger cities of Europe. Others, in search of new opportunities, came to America.

SYNAGOGUE COMPONENTS AND TRADITIONAL REQUIREMENTS

The synagogue is a physical shelter that facilitates the act of Jewish prayer or reading the Torah. The Torah, which is translated as 'law' or 'instruction,' comprises the first five books of the Old Testament, which contain the core teachings of Judaism. Yet Jewish law does not require synagogue buildings for reading the Torah. The minimum criteria are a group of ten Jewish men and certain liturgical elements that are always present in a synagogue; namely, the ark that houses the Torah and the bimah or reading desk (both of which are described in more detail below).

In fact, Jewish texts contain very little information about synagogues' architectural requirements, which is remarkable for a religion so fundamentally based on textual law. By contrast, the Torah is replete with descriptions of the First Temple and the Tabernacle, the portable structure that was used by Moses and the Jews when they were wandering in the desert. The Tabernacle was an A-frame tent that was closed on three sides. Considered the earliest shelter made for worshipping the Jewish God, the Tabernacle's layout prefigured the later architecture of the Temples, in the sense that it contained a series of sacred spaces that were separated by interior courts and curtains. The Torah contains lengthy passages that describe the Tabernacle's exact size, shape, height, and materials, going so far as to explain the exact dimensions and total number of acacia wood planks that were needed to build it.[4]

In contrast, certain regulations have been applied to synagogues at different times and places, but these guidelines have never been universally accepted by the Jewish communities of the Diaspora, nor have they carried over consistently into American synagogue design. For example, in ancient times, Jews were expected to build synagogues on the highest nearby mountaintop or near a body of water, such as a river or a sea. In all likelihood this rule was designed to accommodate the regulations associated with the *mikvah*, or ritual bath, but whatever the basis, this ruling proved impossible to implement over time. Ancient rabbinical prescriptions also dictated that the synagogue should be the tallest building in a city. This requirement was not usually satisfied, as synagogues were often banned from rising higher than neighboring churches. Even when Jews were legally allowed to build tall buildings, they chose to keep structures low in order to avoid appearing ostentatious to their neighbors.

4   Ex. 25–27.

Traditionally, synagogues have been oriented towards Jerusalem. Early rabbis built some flexibility into the rule they formulated: 'In the Diaspora, face the land of Israel; in the Land of Israel, face Jerusalem; in Jerusalem face the Temple Mount.'[5] While this law has not always been followed, it is one of the oldest, best-known synagogue traditions and is still followed by many American congregations today.

Without strict parameters, synagogue design has evolved and changed over the years. Regardless, there is a set of specific architectural elements that are commonly associated with synagogues.

LEFT: *Interior, Altneushul, Prague, 15th century.*
RIGHT: *Ark, Ohef Sholom Synagogue, Norfolk, Virginia (1918).*

BASIC SYNAGOGUE ELEMENTS

Since the medieval period, two basic liturgical elements have governed the space of the sanctuary. These are the ark and bimah. As the focal points of Jewish religious practice, their arrangement in the sanctuary is extremely important. Over the years, Sephardic and Ashkenazi congregations have developed different traditions with regard to their design, decoration, and placement.

The ark—the *aron* (Ashkenazi) or *hechal* (Sephardic)—houses the Torah, the most sacred object in Jewish liturgy and religious life. Before arks existed, the Torah scrolls were brought to the service in portable chests. Given the sanctity of the Torah, the ark—the cabinet that houses the Torah scrolls—is the most essential feature of the synagogue, and it determines the organization of all other elements in the sanctuary. To emphasize the importance of its contents, the ark has traditionally been raised above the main floor of the synagogue and placed along the eastern wall facing

5   Wigoder, p. 36.

Jerusalem. Behind the doors of the ark, a curtain, the *paroket*, makes symbolic reference to the curtain that enclosed the Holy of Holies, the sacred chamber located at the heart of the original Temple in Jerusalem.

The bimah (Ashkenazi), or *tebah* (Sephardic), is the central reading desk, typically made of wood. It is the place where the Torah and other Jewish texts are read aloud during religious services. Traditionally, the bimah has been placed on a separate platform from the ark.

Although not as essential as the ark and bimah, another basic liturgical object is the *ner tamid* or 'eternal light.' This is a continually burning oil lamp, normally made of bronze or brass, which usually hangs above the ark. Symbolically, it represents the light that burned at the ancient Temple.

ICONOGRAPHY, DECORATION, AND JEWISH ART

Historically, Jews have not portrayed human forms in synagogue-related art, because they interpreted the Second Commandment as an injunction against idolatry. This commandment states: 'Thou shalt not make unto thee any graven image, or any likeness of any thing that is in heaven above, or that is in the earth beneath, or that is in the water under the earth.'[6] In ancient times, a strict adherence to this ban clearly distinguished synagogues from other houses of worship, because synagogues were the only religious buildings that lacked idols or shrines in worship of the divine.[7]

Regardless of this prohibition, or perhaps in spite of it, Jews have developed a collection of common religious symbols over the years, and these are frequently used in American synagogues to this day. Certain images, such as the menorah, ram's horn, *lulav* branch, and tablets of the law evolved as common symbols. However, the interpretation of the restriction on idolatry continues to influence the development and content of Jewish art.

The ubiquitous six-pointed Star of David is actually a fairly recent Jewish symbol. Originally connected to Jewish mysticism, its first use can be traced back to a synagogue in the sixth century B.C.E., and the so-called 'Jewish star' did not gain wide acceptance as a universal Jewish symbol until the nineteenth century. It made its first American architectural appearance at the Lloyd Street Synagogue in Baltimore (*page 104*).

Iconography and ornament are now fairly common in American synagogues, although some contemporary congregations have chosen to leave their synagogues devoid of any decoration. The use of Hebrew signage on the exterior of synagogues is itself a kind of iconography, as it identifies the buildings as Jewish. Representational images have even been used in a few liberal American synagogues.

6   Ex. 20: 4.
7   Sed-Rajna, Gabrielle, *Jewish Art*, H.N. Abrams, New York, 1997, p. iii.

The interior layout of the ark, bimah, and seating for worshippers often conveys quite a bit about the kind of service that takes place in a given synagogue sanctuary. In many cases, particular layouts are passed down from generation to generation. Some of these layouts, like the double-nave system that was used in the Altneushul, were originally derived from churches. Over the centuries, these interior arrangements were modified to better accommodate the specific practices of Jewish liturgy.

When early immigrant congregations arrived in America, they often maintained the seating arrangements they had employed in their homelands, even though they largely abandoned the traditional architectural styles of their ancestors. Over time, American congregations rearranged their seating, responding to American influences like the Protestant church. These formal reorganizations paralleled changes in both the liturgy and values of Jewish worshippers.

American sanctuaries are generally based on one of three layouts that developed over the past 500 years. The most common of the three basic configurations is the 'central bimah' plan, so-called because the bimah is placed in the center of the sanctuary to emphasize its significance in the service. In this type of arrangement, the bimah typically faces the eastern wall where the ark is located, and the congregational seating is arranged to face the bimah. This kind of configuration was derived from the rectangular plan of the Roman basilica.

In the most common Sephardic layout, the ark and bimah are placed in the center and face east, and are located at opposite ends of the sanctuary, with an open, central corridor in between. The congregants all sit facing each other along the north and south walls with a central passage between them. We refer to this as the open central aisle plan. In recent variations, the bimah is situated closer to the center of the sanctuary than it is to the western wall, but there is still an open corridor in front of the ark. Although the open central aisle configuration is commonly associated with Sephardic communities, the features of this plan have likely derived from sixteenth-century council chambers in Holland, where a significant number of Sephardim had settled. Its origin may be more ancient, as this type of plan has been used by Sephardic congregations around the world. Some hypothesize that it initially developed in Italy, where it is still used by some of the oldest continuous Jewish communities in the Diaspora. Today, in the United States, this configuration is only found in a few older Sephardic synagogues.

BELOW: The common sanctuary seating arrangements in American synagogues: Central Bimah (left), Open Central Aisle (middle), Theater-style (right).

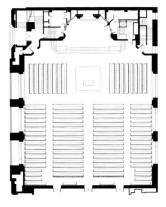
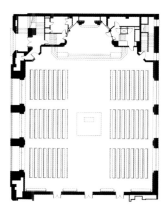
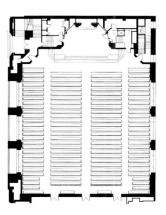

As some American congregations revised their services in response to changing religious values, their seating arrangements followed suit. This gave rise to a third type of plan, the 'theater-style' plan, which has frequently been used in American synagogues. In this seating plan, chairs are oriented to face the bimah and the ark, which are raised on a stage-like platform at the front. The ark here also acts as a podium from which sermons may be read; early Reform congregations first borrowed this configuration from the Protestant church in the middle of the nineteenth century. As these Reform groups continued to adopt the values and culture of American society, they borrowed other ecclesiastical elements as well, perhaps most significantly 'family pews,' which broke with the traditional separation of the sexes in synagogues by allowing men and women to sit together in the sanctuary. This form of seating was thought to establish greater respectability in relation to American society than their previous synagogues provided.[8]

The practice of separating men and women is commonly thought to have originated in the days of the Second Temple, which had separate courts for men and women. However, women's sections did not appear in synagogues until long after the destruction of the Temple, and before that time, women were not expected to attend synagogue services at all.[9] Once they were accepted into houses of prayer, women traditionally sat in galleries or other partitioned areas that were separated by screens or *mechitzahs*. The height and transparency of these *mechitzahs* varied from synagogue to synagogue.

Until recently, most American synagogues were based on one of these three configurations, including Orthodox synagogues that still maintain different seating areas for women and men, a practice that has been discontinued by Conservative and Reform congregations. Reflecting changing attitudes towards the liturgy, a fourth type of configuration is just beginning to emerge in liberal congregations. In order to make services more personal and inclusive, congregations that had previously used theater-style plans are moving the bimah to the center of the sanctuary where it is closer to the congregation. Unlike the traditional arrangement, however, the bimah faces the congregation rather than the ark. Some of these congregations are even opting for moveable seating so that they can arrange their sanctuaries in different ways for specific services and/or special events.

Contemporary Orthodox congregations are also revising their seating patterns. Many have brought women's seating down from the galleries onto the main floor, in order to create a better sense of community among the worshippers. Others are lowering the *mechitzahs* during the non-prayer portions of the service so that all members of the congregation can participate more directly at these times.

8   Detailed evidence of American Jews' quest for respectability in the mid-nineteenth century is shown in Karla Goldman, *Beyond the Synagogue Gallery: Finding a Place for Women in American Judaism*, Harvard University Press, Cambridge, MA, 2000, Chapter 3.

9   Carol Krinsky, *Synagogues of Europe: Architecture, History, Meaning*, Architectural History Foundation, New York; MIT Press, Cambridge, MA, 1985, p. 28.

Throughout history, synagogues have provided social services for Jews who lived in segregation from their neighbors in cities and towns of the Diaspora. Yet it was here in the United States that the synagogue emerged as a modern community center. Ever since the nineteenth century, synagogues have played an expanded role in the life of American Jewish communities. At first, synagogues offered religious and cultural sanctuary for recently arrived Jews. Early synagogues contained study rooms, rabbinical courtrooms, chapels for smaller services, rabbis' studies and other administrative offices, and even apartments for synagogue officials. In recent decades, however, a distinct synagogue type has developed that accommodates expanded religious services, Jewish study, and enhanced social functions. In addition to sacred areas, many contemporary synagogues house a variety of spaces to accommodate myriad occasions: social halls for community and lifecycle events, classrooms for religious schooling and day schools, gift shops, and brides' rooms. Whereas these programmatic elements were once accommodated in lesser areas like basements or annexes, ancillary functions are today taking on greater significance and centrality in the design of contemporary synagogues.

3 | THE AMERICAN SYNAGOGUE

American synagogues document the story of immigrants who arrived in America seeking a better life, succeeded in society, and built prominent and bold edifices in honor of their religion and new civic lives. Whereas European Jews were often restricted to building small, unidentifiable religious buildings within specified districts in their cities and towns, American congregations were able to build in the size, style, and location of their choice. As a physical legacy, these buildings illustrate Jewish communities' struggle to maintain their traditional heritage and Jewish identity while celebrating their acquired American culture.

As they established communities and thrived, American Jews erected synagogues as testaments to their cultural and economic achievements. Many immigrants sought political asylum or an escape from the travails of poverty, segregation, and anti-Semitism that they had suffered in Europe. Others were attracted by the economic opportunity and promise of social mobility that by the middle of the nineteenth century had made the United States the principal destination for emigrant European Jews. While it is true that the first American Jews were not fully protected from anti-Semitism, the spirit of the nation was one of religious tolerance. In 1790, President George Washington confidently wrote to one of the earliest Jewish congregations, the Touro Congregation in Newport, Rhode Island, that the American government 'gives to bigotry no sanction, to persecution no assistance.'

The first American synagogues followed American design trends, just as other Diaspora synagogues had borrowed from local architectures. The earliest immigrants constructed sanctuaries that were concealed in typical vernacular American buildings. Many of them hoped that Judaism would be considered as just another religious denomination among the great number that existed in America, rather than as an

OPPOSITE: *Touro Synagogue, Newport, Rhode Island (1793), the oldest extant synagogue in America.*

ethnic group. Progressive Jewish congregations took cues from the Protestant church: 'family pews' were built, sermons were added to the service, and Sisterhood and Brotherhood groups were formed. In an attempt to assimilate, Jewish congregations emulated Christian values and design elements that they perceived as distinctly American.

In extreme cases, assimilated Jewish congregations left their synagogues so devoid of any Jewish iconography that they were unrecognizable as being 'Jewish' buildings. Other congregations embraced the regional architecture of the places where they settled: the design elements common in Portland, San Francisco, Austin, New York, and the numerous other cities and towns that became home to Jews found their way into American synagogues.

The style and expression of Jewish religious buildings also varied according to how much congregations wanted to conform to mainstream America or distinguish themselves within their local environments. Some retained vestiges of their ethnic heritage, particularly by holding onto traditional seating arrangements and ark and bimah design in the sanctuary. By the same token, some Jews searched for what they considered to be the most 'Jewish' revival styles. A number of styles proliferated, including Greek Revival, Gothic, Egyptian, Romanesque, Moorish, and Byzantine. Models like the Greek temple became very popular, first with Christian congregations and then with Jews. Often traditionally inspired, but rarely historically accurate, this quest for ancestral roots and a sense of belonging remains central to the story of synagogue design in America even today.

Over the past four centuries, American synagogue architecture, having no unified stylistic precedents in history, has often been at the forefront of contemporary American trends, more so than Protestant church design, which has not strayed far from Gothic or Colonial influences.[10] As early as the late nineteenth century, Jewish congregations began to commission designs by some of the most progressive architects, including Peter Harrison, Frank Furness, Frank Lloyd Wright, Adler & Sullivan, and Philip Johnson. In the decades immediately following World War II, Jewish congregations became avid patrons of the avant-garde; hundreds of suburban synagogues were built in modern styles using modern materials. For Jews, this architectural language bespoke a religion that could successfully change along with the American way of life and a community that never faltered in the face of the challenge to continually reinterpret its religious environment.

10 Phillip Johnson, Introduction to *Synagogue Architecture in the United States: History and Interpretation*, by Rachel Witchnitzer, Jewish Publication Society of America, Philadelphia, 1955.

THE FIRST WAVE OF IMMIGRANTS:
SEPHARDIC SYNAGOGUES IN AMERICA

The first Jewish immigrants were of Sephardic origin and arrived in New Amsterdam on a boat from Brazil, nearly a century before the creation of the United States. They were originally from Spain, but had fled in the fifteenth century as a result of the Spanish Inquisition. Facing conversion or even death at home, many found asylum in the Netherlands, and from there they traveled with Dutch traders to South America, Central America, and the American colonies. By the time they arrived in New Amsterdam, they had become important members of Holland's trading industry. Even so, Peter Stuyvesant, the mayor of the New Amsterdam colony at the time, initially refused to welcome the Jews. After some dispute, in 1655 he agreed to allow them to stay under certain conditions, one of which was that they confine the practice their religion to 'their houses.'

The synagogues built by the early Sephardic immigrants were few in number, but they demonstrated the immigrants' social acculturation and validated the Jewish community as an American religious group. Their buildings reflected a balance between two worlds: the immigrants' new home and the cultures of their native countries abroad. In architectural terms, this meant that the internal layouts of these first synagogues were designed to sustain Jewish liturgy, whereas the synagogues' external appearance did not differ markedly from American vernacular traditions in the places where they were built. Many had only one large room with secondary spaces for additional functions like teaching and social events. For the most part, the ark and bimah provided the only clues to these buildings' Jewish identities, and their placement reflected the congregations' Sephardic heritage.

ABOVE: *Sephardic Synagogue, Amsterdam (1675). The floor plan of the Sephardic Synagogue served as a prototype for many early American synagogues.*

Due to Stuyvesant's ban against building synagogues, the first Jews in New Amsterdam originally rented space for their congregation, which they named Congregation Shearith Israel. Nearly 80 years later, Shearith Israel erected the first North American synagogue, the Mill Street Synagogue on Mill Street (since renamed South William Street) in lower Manhattan in 1730. This synagogue was built with financial support from established Sephardic Jewish organizations in Amsterdam and Curaçao, and sat in a neighborhood alongside Dutch, Lutheran, and Baptist churches constructed during the same period. It was a small masonry building that was externally quite indistinguishable from other local structures. Within, the sanctuary's familiar seating arrangement, a typical open central aisle plan with a central bimah and an ark along the east wall, was derived directly from the Sephardic Synagogue in Amsterdam (1675). Men and women were separated: benches for the men ran lengthwise along the north and south walls and women sat in a gallery that lined the synagogue on three sides. The congregation, which is now in its fifth home in New York, continues to use the same seating arrangement to this day.

Another group of Sephardic Jews settled in Rhode Island, the colony founded by Roger Williams in the seventeenth century and a model of religious tolerance. Several decades after the completion of the Mill Street Synagogue, these immigrants built the Touro Synagogue, the oldest existing synagogue in America today. As with the Mill Street Synagogue, the synagogue did not appear 'Jewish.' Rather, its architecture was based directly on a type of local religious building that was popular in and around Newport, Rhode Island: the early eighteenth-century American Congregational meetinghouse. Like most other vernacular buildings in America at the time, almost every detail was inspired by English pattern books. Its façade is decorated with the windows and white trim commonly associated with the Georgian Colonial style; the synagogue is considered to be one of the most important examples of eighteenth-century American architecture (*page 96*).

Like Mill Street and Touro, another early synagogue built by Sephardic immigrants, the Kahal Kadosh Beth Elohim Synagogue (1794), in Charleston, South Carolina, borrowed elements of local architecture in the design of its exterior. Even more significantly, the synagogue's design incorporated details from typical Southern churches, such as the steeple and lantern roof (*page 100*). Inside, however, as at Mill Street, the seating arrangement referred directly to the Sephardic Synagogue in Amsterdam. By the 1840s, when the congregation built its second home, the congregation had become more accustomed to American ways. In its second synagogue, it would eventually replace the open central aisle seating arrangement with the theater-style seating common to the Protestant church.

At the time that the first Kahal Kadosh Beth Elohim Synagogue was built, the Charleston Jewish community was the largest in America. Yet the Jewish New World was still a rather small one. Less than 1500 Jews in all lived in the colonies when the first shots of the American Revolution were fired[11]; even as late as the 1820s, there were just six Jewish congregations in America, in six different cities: New York, Philadelphia, Richmond, Charleston, Savannah, and Newport.

Unlike the later waves of immigrants that arrived in the nineteenth and twentieth centuries, these first immigrants were traders who were already established when they came to America. After several decades, they succeeded economically as merchants in the Dutch, and later British, colonies. For some, acculturation happened so rapidly that they chose to adopt more secular ways of life. These successful, assimilated Jews would have a great impact on the next wave of immigrants who followed closely behind.

ABOVE: *Sanctuary, Kahal Kadosh Beth Elohim, Charleston, South Carolina (1794), which features several traditional Jewish elements, despite its patently American Colonial-style exterior (page 39).*

11 Abraham Karp, *Haven and Home*, Schocken, New York, 1985, pp. 374–75.

The second wave of immigrants came to the United States just as political emancipation was sweeping across Europe. Arriving between 1820 and 1880, this group is referred to by some Jewish historians as the 'German wave' because the majority of immigrants were Ashkenazi Jews from North and Central Europe. The term is something of a misnomer—although Jews from the German states did comprise a slim majority, Jews from Poland, Bohemia, Moravia, Galicia, Alsace, Russia, and Lithuania also made up significant portions of this group. Many of these new immigrants settled in the East Coast cities that were their ports of entry, but some of them spread out, founding entirely new Jewish communities in places as far west as Portland and San Francisco. While they retained ties with Jews from their countries of origin, these immigrants began to form their own congregations, and as they settled into their new homes they looked to vernacular buildings to find inspiration for their new synagogues. Leaving the traditions of their native homelands behind, they built synagogues that expressed their social acceptance in the United States.

Initially, the Ashkenazim joined established Sephardic synagogues, founding their own congregations later on, when their numbers were sufficiently large. Despite their diverse ethnic origins, the Ashkenazi Jews who arrived during the first part of the nineteenth century were united in America by their common immigrant experiences. Many arrived as migrant peddlers, and quickly became successful merchants. Such rags-to-riches stories described many of the new immigrants, and a number of Jewish families (Macy, Guggenheim, and Levi-Strauss to name a few) quickly gained prominence in the New World, both economically and socially. By the 1880s, when droves of Eastern European Jews began migrating to the U.S., the descendants of this German wave of immigrants would be considered well-to-do, and almost unrecognizably assimilated, by those newly arriving.

When building their American synagogues, the Ashkenazim, like other American clients who commissioned civic and religious buildings in the nineteenth century, freely adopted revival styles. In part, this may have been the result of Jews' reliance on non-Jewish architects to design their synagogues until the latter part of the century when Jews began to practice architecture. Immigrant Jews were not usually trained in building because they had been banned from the trade guilds in Europe.

Congregations across America often chose architects who were known for building churches. For instance, when Charleston's Kahal Kadosh Beth Elohim Synagogue burned down in 1838, the congregation replaced it in 1841 with a Classical Revival style synagogue (*page 100*). With a six-column portico and low double-pitched roof, the exterior of the new Beth Elohim was a perfect imitation of a Greek Temple. Though its style may have conveyed its civic or religious importance, it was certainly not 'Jewish.' The architect of Beth Elohim's new building, Cyrus Warner, had designed a church in the same style just two years before.

While it did not look church-like in a traditional sense, Kahal Kadosh Beth
Elohim was built at a time when the Classical Revival style was popular for
ecclesiastical, civic, and institutional buildings throughout the United States.
As a result, these Classical Revival synagogues were easily integrated into their
surroundings, mirroring Jews' social integration in general. This stylistic dress was
common in the South, but it was also popular for synagogues that were built in cities
above the Mason-Dixon line as well. In 1845, the Baltimore Hebrew Congregation
erected a new Classical Revival synagogue that featured an impressive portico with
a triglyph frieze that was supported on four Doric columns.

Congregations could select almost any revival style for the simple purpose of
displaying good taste; rarely was greater meaning attached to a particular choice.
Congregations were not even timid about employing styles that were generally
considered specific to church architecture. For example, in the nineteenth century,
the Gothic Revival style was imported from Europe, and enjoyed popularity in America

ABOVE: *Kahal Kadosh Beth
Elohim, Charleston, South
Carolina (1794), a
synagogue which, with its
slender steeple and pitched
roof, could easily have been
mistaken for a Christian
church. This synagogue was
later replaced by a Neo-
Classical building.*

for a brief time. A number of American synagogues were built in this style, despite its origins in the medieval period and its associations with Christian religious zeal. These synagogues in particular showed how American Jews were eager to maintain connections with their roots while enjoying the freedom to build in whatever style— even blatantly Christian styles—that they desired.

In general, the Gothic Revival style remained less popular than other revival styles, but several representative synagogues were built in American cities. As the city's German congregations began to establish themselves during the 1840s and 1850s, a few Gothic synagogues were built in New York, such as Anshe Chesed (1849) on Norfolk Street and B'nai Jeshuran (1851) on Greene Street. Mikve Israel (1878), in Savannah, Georgia, is a later, more refined example of the Gothic Revival, located directly across from an earlier Gothic edifice that is—not surprisingly—a Protestant church (*page 120*). Further west, a young Jewish community that was forming in San Francisco built its first house of worship in a vernacular Gothic style that was fashioned from wood and included typical details such as pointed arches, buttresses, and pinnacles (see Temple Emanu-El, *page 148*). Apart from the Hebrew inscriptions placed above its entranceways, it was scarcely possible to distinguish the building from a Gothic church.

During the age of revivalism, Jews began to develop elements of a distinctly American Jewish iconography that was integrated into the design of synagogues throughout the United States. While revivalism as an interpretative practice afforded architects a certain amount of stylistic leeway, Jewish symbolism was often quite distinct when it appeared in the context of American buildings. For example, the round, multi-colored window above the ark in the Baltimore Hebrew Congregation's Lloyd Street Synagogue departed radically from the typical vocabulary of the Classical style (*page 104*). More significantly, the center of the stained-glass window formed a six-pointed Star of David. This emergent universal sign of Judaism was probably used here in an American synagogue for the first time, and it demonstrated the importance of Jewish symbolism in an American building whose style was otherwise quite typical of the time.

OPPOSITE: *B'nai Jeshuran, New York, New York (1851), which was designed in the Gothic Revival style, despite the fact that Gothic architecture was primarily associated with the Christian church.*

The use of Jewish iconography in the Lloyd Street Synagogue may have been only a token expression of Jewish identity, but it points to changes in American synagogues as Jewish congregations began to debate questions of prominence and style. By the mid- to late-nineteenth century, Jewish communities throughout the United States started to question what American synagogues should look like and what purposes they should serve in the community. This was a complex search, encompassing as it did so many issues at once. In part, it illustrated the need for Jewish communities to define their identities in local American contexts, to construct distinguished synagogues as a way to build pride among their congregants, or even to appeal to unaffiliated Jews. In major cities across the United States, growing American congregations built larger and more prominent synagogues, such as New York's Temple Emanu-El of 1868, which has since been demolished (*page 43*). Because these new synagogues represented Jews' social arrival in America, they were also the physical and visual symbols of a friendly rivalry among Jewish congregations as they vied for social status in the United States.

ABOVE: *Lloyd Street Synagogue, Baltimore, Maryland (1845).*

Considering that Jews throughout history had adopted regional and local styles, it was especially difficult to define an authentically 'Jewish' architecture. Apart from borrowed European styles and certain decorative symbols, Jewish ancient history, while a source of pride and the wellspring of Jews' religious and cultural identity, had long been inaccessible to synagogue designers. At this point, the architecture of the earliest synagogues in the Holy Land was virtually unknown.

In the nineteenth century, American architects began to question what might constitute an authentic Jewish style, partially as an outgrowth of contemporary European discussions about the appropriate style or styles for synagogues. These debates emerged in the context of wider discussions about proper styles for ecclesiastical architecture, coinciding with the rise of the Gothic Revival, hailed as the only 'true' Christian style by a cadre of European revivalists including Augustus Pugin, Viollet-le-Duc, and John Ruskin.

ABOVE: *Temple Emanu-El, New York, New York (1868), was considered the most impressive synagogue in its day.*

This period also witnessed the emergence of the first Jewish architects who were considered to be sensitive to the particular needs and tastes of American Jews. The first known Jewish architect in America was Leopold Eidlitz (1823–1908) who designed several synagogues and churches in New York City, as well as a variety of buildings throughout New England.

Eidlitz's Wooster Street Synagogue (1847) for the Shaaray Tefila congregation in New York encapsulates the debate over architecture and Jewish identity. For the Wooster Street synagogue, Eidlitz employed the Romanesque Revival style, which contemporaries referred to as 'Byzantic.' This architectural style had been used frequently in Germany but never for an American synagogue. Samuel M. Isaacs, *hazan* (reader) at the Shaaray Tefila congregation, hailed the synagogue as a distinctly Jewish building, commenting in the Jewish monthly *The Occident* that

'...the style chosen is the Byzantic, which flourished some centuries back, and was especially used by the Portuguese and other Jews when persecuted in the middle ages; the imposing grandeur of the style, together with its Oriental origin...will render it best adapted for a building of this class and character...the spectator will at once receive the impression that the building is intended for a place of worship, not of the poetical deities of the Greeks, nor the pompous trinity of the Christians, but of the mighty God of the Jews.'[12]

Isaacs' review sanctioned Jews to claim affinity, like their Christian counterparts, with a certain architectural style in a symbolic and meaningful way. In the years that followed, the Romanesque Revival or 'Byzantic' style became one of the first revival styles in America to be successfully aligned with past Jewish history.

During this period, architects began to turn their attention toward the emerging science of archaeology, for further information on what styles might be historically and ideologically appropriate for various building types. This marked a change for architects and Jewish congregations that had made choices among different stylistic revivals based for the most part on taste, or on impressionistic historical analyses like those provided by Isaacs.

After 1865, significant archeological discoveries by the Palestine Exploration Fund (PEF) invigorated the search for a Jewish style. Formed by a group of British archeologists, academics, and clergymen, the PEF undertook an investigation of the history of ancient Israel and the Levant (the eastern Mediterranean region). Their excavations in Palestine shed new light on early Jewish architecture and provided information that could be incorporated in contemporary Jewish structures. Most notably, the PEF uncovered ancient synagogues that had used Classical motifs. The news of these findings spawned many Classical Revival synagogues towards the end of the nineteenth century, including some Eastern European synagogues in Harlem and a new home for Shearith Israel in New York (*page 132*). Although the Classical Revival style had previously been used for synagogues in Charleston and Baltimore, it had never carried symbolic weight. But architect Arnold Brunner chose this design for Shearith Israel precisely because of the archaeological revelation that Classical forms had been used in early synagogues. Later, at the turn of the century, when Byzantine-influenced synagogues such as the synagogue at Bet Alfa were uncovered in Palestine, the revelation inspired the construction of Byzantine-style synagogues across the country.

Along with the PEF expeditions, the experiences of colonialism and European imperialism were powerful influences on European and American architects, who became increasingly fascinated with exotic lands and cultures. European architects subsequently began to experiment with non-Western forms, and in time, they would go on to create new interpretations of older religious styles.

12 S.M Isaacs, 'Of the New Synagogue, Now Building at New York, for the Congregation under the Pastoral Charge of the Rev. S. M. Isaacs,' *The Occident* 4, no. 5, August 1846, pp. 239–240.

The search for a quintessential Jewish architecture that began with the Byzantic or Romanesque Revival culminated with the Moorish style. It seemed to best capture the two-fold sense of acceptance and exclusion that underscored the social experience of American Jews. If any building style found universal favor as distinctively 'Jewish,' surely this was it. Moorish architecture resonated with the Jews because they had long been perceived as an 'Other,' alluding equally to their origins in the East as well as their exclusion from mainstream society in their adopted countries—even in the United States. The use of the Moorish style conveyed a dual message: on the one hand, Jews proudly proclaimed their otherness from American society by using a pastiche of Eastern architectural traditions; on the other hand, the use of the popular Moorish style—a mix of influences, Jewish and otherwise—was a bridge between Jews' religious heritage and American society.

In fact, the Moorish style was not a 'true' revival style because it did not refer directly to one type of architecture. Rather, it was a European invention, standing for an eclectic blend of Islamic, Byzantine, and Oriental elements that drew upon European colonial experiences in the Near and Middle East. European architects employed the Moorish style for a variety of civic building types, including synagogues. From Europe, the style was exported to the United States in the second half of the nineteenth century, and was often used in cases where designers wanted to evoke a feeling of wonder and a sense of occasion. This otherworldliness was embodied in the Crystal Palace that was erected for the New York World's Fair in 1853, a majestic building topped with a Saracenic dome, minarets, and parapets in the form of arabesques. The style became fashionable, and remained so through the early decades of the twentieth century. It was employed for a variety of building types—turn-of-the-century theaters and cinema houses, for example, were commonly decorated with Moorish motifs and eastern pattern-work, feeding Americans' taste for exotic, tantalizing architecture.

Although the Moorish style's design traditions did have historic relevance for Sephardic communities that had lived in Muslim countries, it was ironically the Ashkenazi Jews in Europe who most wholeheartedly embraced this style. When the renowned German architect Gottfried Semper used elaborate patterns from the Alhambra—an Islamic palace of fourteenth-century Spain—for a synagogue in Dresden, it was interpreted as reference to the non-Western 'otherness' of the Jews. Semper's student Otto Simonson later adapted these ideas for a synagogue in Leipzig. By the 1850s, Moorish synagogues were appearing all over Europe. It is ironic, but perhaps not surprising, that Europeans would call attention to the strangeness of the Jews at a time when they were starting to enjoy greater civil and religious rights.

In America, Moorish architecture became fashionable even as it was equated with things that were foreign, mysterious, and strange. Since it was popular in secular society, Jews' use of the style signaled that they were part of the larger community—that they were American—but at the same time made clear that they desired to express their Semitic heritage, so long as it was accepted by the general public. Rabbi Isaac Wise, the galvanizing force behind the American Reform movement, was one of the first to advocate the use of the Moorish style for an American congregation, in Cincinnati's Plum Street Temple of 1866 (*page 108*). Wise wrote that the synagogue was designed 'in the Byzantine style, with steeples and several minor towers...The building according to the plan will be truly grand both in design and dimensions.'[13] Though the synagogue was in fact a Gothic building decorated with Oriental motifs, when it was finished Wise called it an 'Alhambra Temple.' By associating the Moorish-style Plum Street Temple with the iconic Islamic palace, which was widely revered for its architecture, Wise was insisting that it embodied a perfect style of synagogue design. In addition, allusions to the Alhambra nostalgically recalled Jews' period of coexistence with other religious groups in Muslim-ruled Spain.

ABOVE: *Exterior view (rear), Plum Street Temple, Cincinnati, Ohio (1866). The synagogue's pointed minaret towers indicate the burgeoning popularity of the Moorish style for American synagogues.*

13 Isaac M. Wise, *The Israelite*, 6 May 1864, quoted in Rachel Witchinzer, *Synagogue Architecture in the United States*, pp. 70–72.

In 1868, New York's leading Reform congregation, Emanu-El, followed Plum
Street's lead. The congregation commissioned Eidlitz and Henry Fernbach to build
a Moorish synagogue for its prominent new home. Exotic, lacy decoration on the
exterior of the building and its towers gave the structure an Oriental feel. Inside the
sanctuary, abstract ornamental patterns rendered in colors like red, blue, yellow, white,
and gold spread across the great expanses of the walls. Other notable Moorish-
influenced synagogues include New York City's Central Synagogue (1872) and
Eldridge Street Synagogue (1886) (*pages 112 and 122*), and Gemiluth Chassed in Port
Gibson, Mississippi (1892) (*page 126*); all illustrate the widespread prevalence of the
Moorish style among Jewish congregations throughout America. Earlier homes of
Temple Emanu-El in San Francisco and Temple Beth Israel in Portland were also built
in the Moorish style (*pages 148 and 152*).

Despite its use in secular building, the Moorish style never became quite as
popular for synagogues in America as it did in Europe. Perhaps, in America, Jews felt
more accepted by their peers and therefore felt less of a need to express their social
and religious emancipation through the choice of particular architectural styles. In
other words, Jews did not have to use exotic, non-Western forms to express their faith;
they were comfortably part of two communities—one Jewish, one American—and they
could simply enjoy the profound freedom of being unique.

JEWISH IDENTITY AND AMERICAN LITURGY

As the American Jewish population increased dramatically during the nineteenth
century, the practice of Judaism began to change, and with it the form that its houses
of worship would take. In 1820, when the second wave of immigration began, there
were 2700 Jews in America. When this wave ended around 1880, the number had
climbed to 250,000, an increase of nearly a hundredfold. Over the next 40 years,
the Jewish population nearly doubled each decade. By the time the third wave of
immigration finished around 1920, there were nearly 3,600,000 Jews living in the
United States.[14]

This century-long period of growth had a lasting effect on Jewish liturgy,
including the development of innovative new religious affiliations. The rise of the
American Reform Movement was one of the earliest examples. It was separate, and
slightly different, from the Reform movement in Germany, although they are
commonly assumed to be one and the same. The latter movement developed at the
beginning of the nineteenth century, as emancipated German Jews adopted many
of the secular values of the European Enlightenment. But even before the German
Jews arrived in America, an indigenous Reform Movement was beginning to emerge
in response to mainstream religious practices. Its founders were members of the Kahal
Kadosh Beth Elohim congregation in Charleston who strongly desired to create a new
kind of Judaism that synthesized modern values with Jewish traditions. Like their
Christian and Catholic brethren in America, they petitioned to pray in a language they

OPPOSITE: *Central
Synagogue, New York,
New York (1868). This
synagogue's twin bulbous
domes added an exotic
touch to the New York
City skyline.*

14 Karp, 374–75.

could understand. They split with their congregation and organized the first Reform congregation in the United States, the Reformed Society of Israelites. Congregants rejected the physical symbols of cultural segregation such as prayer shawls (*tallit*) and skullcaps (*kippot*). In this way, they suggested that Judaism was an established American creed, rather than a separate religion or race. It was the beginning of a steady progression. By 1881, some 90 percent of the 200 major American congregations were affiliated with the Reform movement.

Reform Judaism contributed to a transformation of synagogue architecture in America. Reform Jews especially admired the respectability and formality that the Protestant churches conveyed. They began to call their synagogues 'temples,' and in so doing they announced that Jews no longer had to wait for the rebuilding of the Temple in Jerusalem. They permanently incorporated the Christian tradition of the sermon into their services, and in their synagogues they moved the bimah to the eastern end of the sanctuary, to emphasize this new aspect of the weekly Shabbat service. These theater-style seating arrangements, replacing the open central aisle and central bimah plan, became the norm.

The reformers owed their success to the social and religious tolerance that allowed Jews to become acculturated members of American society. But for Jewish immigrants of the first and second waves, the Reform Movement was a means of religious survival, because the same liberal conditions that facilitated Jewish integration into mainstream society also threatened the existence of Judaism itself, as they placed Jews' traditional practices at odds with modernity.

The Reform Movement is only part of the story of the American Jews. In response to the liberal reforms taking place in many American congregations, those who held on to traditional practices organized their own institutions, giving birth to the Orthodox movement in the United States. By 1890, following a decade of mass immigration by Eastern European Jews, Orthodox congregations comprised the majority of American congregations. The new arrivals preferred traditional Judaism to the practices of American Reform, which they found totally foreign.

Later, Jews who sought to meld the old with the new, while maintaining the traditions of observant Jewish life, founded a third affiliation. In 1913, the Conservative Movement was established with the formation of the United Synagogues of America. A few decades later, rabbi and philosopher Mordecai Kaplan began developing the tenets of Reconstructionist Judaism, the fourth Jewish affiliation. In the generations to come, Jewish congregations would be defined less by their ethnic roots or country of origin—Germany, Russian, Poland, or Spain—than by their affiliation with one of these four branches of Judaism.

The most dramatic story of arrival unfolded with the third and final wave of immigrant Jews who arrived between 1881 and 1924 (in 1924 the United States passed legislation that drastically curtailed immigration). The great majority of American Jewry descends from this group of two million immigrants, almost all of whom hailed from Eastern Europe. Initially, the arrival of these Eastern European Jews called into question the institutions and practice of American Jewry. In contrast to the previous two waves of immigrants, this third wave of Jews arrived at a time when hundreds of American congregations and Jewish institutions, such as the Young Men's Hebrew Association (YMHA) and B'nai Brith, already existed. This Jewish infrastructure helped to ease the integration of the Eastern European Jews into American society, even given their differences with more assimilated American Jews, especially Reform Jews whom they first encountered in the United States. After a time, the new immigrants were able to create their own congregations, and they eventually built impressive synagogue buildings that proclaimed their social arrival as they relocated from inner-city ghettos to more affluent urban districts.

At first, however, like the Sephardic and German immigrants before them, the Eastern European Jews built synagogues that reflected the ways in which they tempered the acculturation process with the values and traditions of their homelands. Wherever they settled, Eastern European immigrants created *shteiblach*, or one-room synagogues, which contrasted sharply with the large, elaborate American synagogues that surrounded them. While existing American Jewish congregations were becoming more and more defined by religious affiliation than shared ethnic roots, the new immigrants organized *landsmanshaftn*, groups whose members came from the same towns and villages in Eastern Europe. Hundreds of *landsmanshaftn* appeared across America; they acted as cultural and spiritual centers that gave Jews from similar backgrounds some measure of control over the process of Americanization. Their *shteiblach* were anything but opulent; in most cases, they were unadorned rooms containing an ark, a reading table, chairs, and bookcases. By contrast, successive generations would build some of the most dazzling synagogues in the United States.

The prevalence of Orthodoxy among these congregations often had more to do with the immigrants' cultural and ethnic heritage than their religious piety. In fact, the Eastern European Jews were truly considered an 'oriental race,' even by some middle-class American Jews who rallied behind impressive philanthropic efforts to alleviate the social problems of the immigrants by giving aid for education and housing. Others worried privately that the immigrants' poverty would soil the social status that the first two waves of American Jews had fought so hard to win.

One of the most long-lasting legacies of this wave of Jewry was the vibrant Yiddish culture (*Yiddishkeit*) that thrived in the dense enclaves of major American cities such as New York, Chicago, Boston, and Baltimore for over four decades. Without a doubt, Manhattan's Lower East Side was the center of this new phenomenon. In a city where three out of four people were born on foreign soil, the Jews constituted their own majority on the island of Manhattan's eastern tip.

Life was both exciting and trying for these Jews who lived in a world of overpopulated tenements, congested streets, and dangerous workplaces. For decades, the *shtieblach* established by the *landsmanshaftn* served as centers of religious activity, dominating Jewish life on the Lower East Side. East Broadway became known as 'Shtiebl Row' because so many one- and two-room synagogues or *shtieblach* were concentrated on this street. These storefront shuls were more than houses of worship: they hosted seminars, labor discussions, and other secular activities. The *landsmanshaftn* operated as mutual aid societies with vast networks of support, providing a variety of social services such as medical care, burial arrangements, and relief for the poor.

The first synagogue to be built from the ground up by Eastern European Jews was New York's Eldridge Street Synagogue (*page 122*); most congregations had been forced to worship in tiny, converted spaces wherever they could be acquired. When the Eldridge Street Synagogue was built, it declared the congregation's economic success in relation to the older, more established Jewish communities in New York. Though most congregations held steadfastly to their shared ethnic roots, this one was a bit of an anomaly because its members hailed from various regions of Eastern Europe. Interestingly, the synagogue's architecture blended the styles that were most commonly associated with Jewish American identity, the Moorish and the Romanesque. Other Jewish iconography was used extensively along with Russian-style finials that were probably inspired by the church architecture in some of the congregants' homelands. This was only the first of many, many synagogues that were subsequently built on the Lower East Side.

Later, when New York's Eastern European Jews began to move uptown, working-class Jews built modest shuls like those of the Lower East Side. Meanwhile, their middle-class counterparts constructed more opulent synagogues in central Harlem that proudly proclaimed their upward social mobility. Like the synagogues built by the Germans who preceded them by a generation, these new edifices were predominantly revivalist: some were neo-classical, some Romanesque, and others were more eclectic still. But nearly all of them conveyed an energetic sense of dignity and an unapologetic grandeur. They were striking, but not overtly Jewish. As architectural critic David Dunlap writes, the four stout Corinthian columns of Arnold Brunner's Temple Israel (1905) in Harlem 'could be mistaken for Imperial Rome were it not for the Stars of David nestled in their capitals.'[15]

15 David Dunlap, 'Vestiges of Harlem's Jewish Past,' *The New York Times*, 7 June 2002.

From the Lower East Side, then to East Harlem, Jews later followed prominent families to the Upper East and West Sides and built grand synagogues. Since that time, many of the Harlem synagogues have been converted into African–American churches, including some of the country's most prominent. Back on the Lower East Side, many former Eastern European synagogues have also been adapted to other uses, such as churches and performance spaces. They still stand as the last remnants of the days when the Lower East Side was predominantly Jewish.

1920S AMERICA

Despite the differences between the three major branches of Judaism, by the 1920s congregations of all types and affiliations had built synagogues that bore witness to Jews' loyalty to their own communities, as well as their acceptance of American ways of life.

Two centuries after the completion of America's first synagogue, many Jewish congregations had the influence and wealth to build impressive edifices demonstrating that religious freedom and economic prosperity were compatible in the United States. One of the best examples is the 1897 construction of a fifth synagogue for Congregation Shearith Israel, the same congregation that built the first American synagogue, the Mill Street Synagogue. More than 150 years later, the congregation's social mobility had earned it a dazzling new home, designed by distinguished Jewish-American architect Arnold Brunner, at a chic address on New York's famous Central Park West (*page 132*).

American synagogues not only became more impressive, but they also got larger and more prominent. In 1929, Congregation Emanu-El in New York built the largest synagogue in the world, a title that it maintains to this day. It was the fifth home for a congregation that had been established more than 75 years earlier by German immigrants on New York's Lower East Side. Meanwhile, on the other side of the country, Reform Temple Beth Israel (1928) of Portland, Oregon inaugurated its third home: a majestic edifice that is known as one of the finest regional examples of the Byzantine Revival style and is listed on the National Register of Historic Places (*page 152*). Members of the congregation included some of the most respected civic leaders of Portland and the state of Oregon.

After the 1920s, building activity began to wane. Few synagogues were built in the 1930s and the 1940s during the Depression and the Second World War, and when construction did resume, synagogues had changed functionally as well as formally. These changes were the result of shifting demographics in the United States. Jewish communities followed other middle-class Americans who were leaving the urban centers of America. As a result, synagogues began to crop up in the outlying suburbs. Mostly out of necessity, Jewish houses of worship were evolving in a new direction from the urban synagogues of the past. As they began to fashion new lifestyles and new Jewish identities, Jews established new synagogues with such a fervor that it ushered in a striking evolution in American Jewry. Once again, the American synagogue was about to be reborn.

In stark contrast to the 1930s, the years following World War II saw a flood of new synagogue construction in the United States. By 1949, over 1800 new American synagogues were in the works, in a construction boom that paralleled the process of suburbanization that began after the Second World War. So many Jews moved to the suburbs that this shift could almost be considered a wave of immigration in its own right; this 'wave' ushered in greater changes in the design of American synagogues than any of the previous three waves of immigration had done. Demographic changes aside, the rise in synagogue construction can be seen, at least partially, as a response to the Holocaust. American Jews sought catharsis, a way to process the horror inflicted upon their relatives and fellow Jews and to create something new in response. By establishing new houses of worship, they reaffirmed their ethnic backgrounds and renewed their Jewish identity as individuals and as a people.

By the end of the War, Jews had certainly arrived in the United States both economically and professionally, but for the most part they lived in multi-family housing in urban Jewish communities. Like other Americans, Jews left urban centers in the 1940s and 1950s, propelled by the popularity of the automobile, new roads, and shortages in urban housing. The move to the suburbs was an important step for Jews because it allowed them to keep pace with the changing definition of what it meant to be a full-fledged American—and by the 1950s, that definition had come to include ownership of a home. More affluent Jews moved to older suburbs that did not have adequate Jewish populations to support active synagogues, while others took up residency in new tract developments. In both instances, new suburban synagogues had to replace a multitude of urban institutions and services. In addition to the three historic functions of the synagogue—prayer, study, and assembly—new ancillary facilities helped to fill the need for Jewish support systems in the suburbs.

The transformation of synagogues into community centers for Jewish cultural and social life is a uniquely American phenomenon. More significantly, these new suburban synagogues became Jewish community centers in a way that only a few of the urban synagogues had ever been; they included, beyond the sacred spaces, a range of functions such as religious schools, social halls, libraries, gift shops, and youth lounges. The assembly and study functions of American synagogues were expanded on an unprecedented scale, and their educational, social, and community functions received greater emphasis. Classrooms and social halls, which had once been relegated to stuffy, windowless basements, were moved to ground floors, and sometimes placed in their own separate wings.

Whereas in the past, many synagogues had been entered via impressive arrival sequences that opened into the sanctuaries, these grand entrances were replaced with more informal lobbies. While the change was functional—from the new lobbies, members had access to the functions dispersed throughout the synagogue's various annexes—it was also driven by the new dependence on the automobile. As most congregants now arrived by car, synagogues' formal street entrances were transferred to back entries, often located next to parking lots. Orthodox Jews did not drive on the Sabbath, so their suburban communities tended to remain closer and more tightly knit.

As synagogues drew larger numbers of congregants, the interior layouts of their sanctuaries needed to change. Most new synagogues were built on theater-style seating plans, but the concept of internal flexibility began to play a major part in design. Differing demands meant flexible organizations that could accommodate various spatial requirements. The number of worshippers differed widely, depending on the occasion. Certain occasions, such as the High Holy Days, drew far more congregants than others. To accommodate these fluctuations in attendance, architects were challenged to find flexibility in their new synagogue designs.

As early as 1907, one Jewish architect, Albert Kahn, started to experiment with folding doors as a way to expand seating in the main sanctuary as might often be required. Several decades later, similar studies were completed by Percival Goodman, a Jewish architect and the designer of more than 50 modern synagogues, making him the most prolific synagogue designer in American history. Recognizing the need for flexibility, Goodman developed schemes for modern synagogues that included folding doors, partitions, and walls that opened into social halls or lounge areas so that the sanctuaries could be expanded for larger services on the High Holy Days. These ideas formed the basis of the designs for two of his early synagogues, West End Synagogue (1952) in Nashville, Tennessee, and Beth El Synagogue in Providence, Rhode Island, completed in 1955 (*page 178*).

A NEW STYLE: THE MODERN SYNAGOGUE

ABOVE: *Park Synagogue,*
Cleveland Heights, Ohio
(1953).

Because American synagogues had never been standardized, Jews were freer than
other religious groups to experiment with vanguard ideas in design. In fact, Jewish
congregations were some of the first clients to embrace modern architecture in
America just as it was beginning to be sanctioned for civic, institutional, and religious
buildings. From the beginning, progressive Jewish architects led the way. Eric
Mendelsohn, a German-born architect who emigrated to America in the 1930s,
stated the case for modern architecture quite clearly: 'It has been said that religious
structures must be traditional in order to impart a sense of the sacred and that the
dignity and emotional significance of such buildings can only be expressed through
historical association. To admit this is to deny that religion is an important part of
our contemporary society.'[16] Although the argument is a strong one, the choice of
the modern style was influenced by other factors as well.

While nineteenth- and early twentieth-century congregations had looked to
history for forms that would express an authentic sense of Jewish identity while fitting
into the American scene, modern buildings were associated with idealistic values that
connoted a new, fresh, and utopian life. They were clean, bright, and logical; their

16 Eric Mendelsohn, in *Recent*
American Synagogue Architecture,
Jewish Theological Seminary of
America and the Jewish Museum,
New York, 1963, p. 23.

simple, straightforward designs resonated with the Jewish families who settled in the suburbs and were eager to demonstrate their new social status in a prominent and visible way. For Jewish intellectuals, life in the suburbs represented their professional achievements and their acceptance into occupations that had been closed to them in the past. For less affluent and first-generation Jews, the suburbs fulfilled the dreams of a different life, better schools for their children, and new homes. These Jews were particularly keen to break their ties with existing urban synagogues that were old, cramped, and bore the stigma of the insular urban ethnic neighborhoods from which they had fled.

Putting revival styles aside, Jews created new prototypes for synagogues that relied on innovation and invention, rather than traditional or Christian models of design. The new suburban synagogues came without any stylistic precedents attached. Freed from the restrictions of fitting new buildings into tight urban grids, architects now had the opportunity to design buildings as freestanding structures within the surrounding landscape. Given this newfound freedom, synagogue architects began to experiment with modern sculptural forms.

For the first time in the history of the synagogue, modern architecture nurtured the emergence of religious design that was distinctly American yet authentically Jewish. Architects searched for new forms and materials to express the spirituality of the Jews in built form. While it is true that some Christian churches also began to sport modernist designs, the initial acceptance of avant-garde architectural styles for synagogues was more rapid. Post-war architects employed the style and vocabulary of modern or international style architecture at the same time that they began to reinterpret conventional building types. As modernism began to take hold, religious spaces became more abstracted but no less meaningful.

The modern style offered the efficiency, economy, and flexibility that these new buildings required. Jewish congregations in the suburbs had to start from scratch and needed to build new buildings quickly. From the outset, modern architecture proved most able to accommodate these multiple requirements and demands. Modern architecture combined simple materials in a straightforward fashion that satisfied clients' budgets as well as their programs and goals.

Two distinct versions of the modern synagogue have since emerged. The first type draws upon the straightforward, institutional type of modernism that is common in educational and public architecture; applied Jewish art and decoration give this kind of unadorned, simple building its particular religious appeal. The second type is heroic or metaphorical in tone, and it relies on the use of detail pertaining to symbolic and abstract motifs. In certain cases, the entire form of these synagogue buildings evokes a particular biblical reference or symbol such as the shape of a six-pointed star.

The first type of modern synagogue design—simple, straightforward, and
unpretentious—largely reflected the civic and institutional architecture of the 1950s,
expressed in building complexes like the new suburban public schools. It featured
open, utilitarian spaces with smooth surfaces, and little, if any, ornamentation; as in
other modern buildings in America, new materials and finishes like glass, metals, and
wood paneling were introduced. The architecture was not inherently 'Jewish,' but
spirituality was conveyed through the insertion of Jewish liturgical objects and art
such as stained-glass windows, menorahs, arks, and sculptures.

Percival Goodman is often credited with disseminating this type of modern
synagogue, and with good reason: many of his design concepts had an enormous
influence on the design and organization of synagogues that were built in the post-war
period throughout the United States. For years, prior to working on synagogues, he
studied ways to redefine notions of community planning and methods of stimulating
active use. He felt that it was particularly important to bring Jewish communities
together in the suburbs, where they had become much more dispersed than they
had been in urban centers.

Goodman did not want the architecture of his synagogues to overshadow the
practice of the liturgy. Instead, he gave equal importance to the educational, social,
and religious elements of his designs. For him, education and community were as
sacred as prayer; all three functions were given equal value, because he believed that
'our religion, unlike the Christian, is horizontal: all is holy, the temple, the home,
the mountain, and the valley. The Christian concept is vertical: from a point on the
ground, man aspires to God. So all is profane except this aspiration. Our faith makes
it possible for me to design the social part, the educational parts and the worship as
a unity for all our activities shall be a hymn in His praise.'[17]

Goodman's synagogues established a successful prototype that was widely
adopted by congregations throughout the United States. This prototype generally took
the form of a low-rise, horizontal building that was entered though a central lobby
(often with an adjacent courtyard) which led to classrooms, a social hall, and a
sanctuary. Although he sought to create a type of architecture that was different from
the church, Goodman utilized the theater-style seating plans that American Jews had
adopted from Protestant churches. Sanctuaries were designed so that services could be
conducted more like theater productions than participatory events. Goodman's
sanctuaries were also somewhat insular and secluded from the world outside. More
often than not, windows were obscured with art or glass, or else they were so elevated
as to preclude any glimpses of outdoor views.

But modern design was not enough to separate Goodman's synagogues from
churches or mosques. Although their materials and massing were simple, Goodman's
synagogues served as a neutral backdrop for applied decoration and objects that
established Jewish references and themes. In fact, the emergence of modern
architecture paralleled the rise of a self-conscious Jewish art within American

17 Percival Goodman, 'The New
Synagogue,' October 1953,
manuscript, quoted in Kimberly
J. Elman 'The Quest for
Community: Percival Goodman
and the Design of the Modern
Synagogue' in *Percival Goodman:
architect, planner, teacher, painter*,
Columbia, New York, p. 58.

synagogues. Goodman brought in artists and sculptors to create appropriate objects that would enhance the synagogue experience in uniquely Jewish ways.

The integration of artwork was a radically new approach. For centuries, Jews had shied away from artistic representation because iconography in the synagogue was banned. After the war, many more artists started to specialize in Judaica and create artwork that exclusively addressed Jewish themes. Most of this ecclesiastical art was large-scale and site-specific. Some of the best work was executed by established artists: Louise Nevelson, well-known for her sculptural reliefs, was commissioned to design an ark for the congregation of Temple Emanuel in Great Neck, New York; in 1960, Temple Beth Zion in Buffalo invited the renowned artist Ben Shahn to design the stained-glass windows flanking the ark. It has since become commonplace for congregations to commission artists to design key elements of synagogues, such as arks and stained-glass windows, as well as other decorative pieces.

NEW SYMBOLISM

In addition to Goodman's model for post-war American synagogues, a second category of modern synagogues developed over time. By the 1960s, new approaches to design were changing the modern style, as buildings became more sculptural and new structural forms and different kinds of natural and man-made materials were introduced. The result was a 'heroic' model for synagogues that was distinguished by awe-inspiring spaces combining structural bravura with artistic flair. This type of architecture spoke directly to Jews' survival after the Holocaust and the founding of the State of Israel in 1948.

ABOVE: *Stained glass windows by Ben Shahn at Temple Beth Zion, Buffalo, New York (1966).*

BELOW: *Kneses Tifereth*
Israel, Port Chester,
New York (1956).

This period of American architectural history, a time when many new schools of design began to emerge, is often called late modernism. Architects began to focus their attention on creating more abstract, monumental spaces to evoke a sense of awe. These architects enjoyed the paradox of using the overtly rational practices of modern architecture and engineering in order to create buildings whose religious functions, by definition, surpassed the mundane parameters of reason. In 1967, architect Marcel Breuer described the current mood: 'Modest as it may be, a place of worship seems to demand dignity and serenity as its birthright. It is part of its function to reach beyond function. Its destiny seems to be to express in static material—stone, concrete, glass— man's drive towards the spiritual.'[18]

Wealthy suburban Jewish communities commissioned leading American architects to create modern, monumental synagogues that could express their stature in America and their desire to reaffirm their Jewish identities in the post-war world. Major American architects (both Jewish and non-Jewish), including Frank Lloyd Wright, Minoru Yamasaki, Eric Mendelssohn, Louis Kahn, and Max Abramovitz, designed synagogues.

Late in his career, Frank Lloyd Wright designed the Beth Shalom Synagogue (1954) in Elkins Park, Pennsylvania (*page 174*). Fifty years earlier, he had completed the Unity Temple in Oak Park, Illinois, which is considered to be one of the first modern religious buildings. In Unity Temple, built for a philosophically progressive

18 Marcel Breuer, in *Recent American Synagogue Architecture*, p. 19.

Unitarian congregation anxious for a design that broke with tradition, Wright deliberately rejected traditional church design, writing: 'Was not...the church steeple, pointing on high, a misleading symbol perhaps? Was not the time come now to be more simple, to put more faith in man on his earth and less anxiety concerning his Heaven about which he could *know* nothing?'[19]

The Elkins Park synagogue is equally unconventional, but more abstract and much more imposing than the Unity Temple. The soaring profile of the Elkins Park Synagogue seems to rival the vertical thrust of the Gothic cathedral, but it could never be mistaken for a church. Wright insisted that the design had a purely Jewish-inspired symbolism. The pyramid-like shape of the building was meant to embody, as Wright called it, 'a traveling Mount Sinai.'

Other American architects designed powerful, assertive architectural statements that reflected the confidence of the American Jews for whom they were designed. Philip Johnson's Kneses Tifereth Israel (1956) in Port Chester, New York, is a crisp juxtaposition of geometric forms (*page 180*). In 1963, Minoru Yamasaki, best known for New York City's World Trade Center, made subtle reference to Middle Eastern themes and shapes in his design for the North Shore Congregation Israel (1964) of Glencoe, Illinois (*page 192*). By inserting a spectacular pinnacle form into the local landscape, he used the power of technology to heighten the community's awareness of an uplifting and holy space. And in Marcel Breuer's Westchester Reform Temple in Scarsdale, New York, the building itself is molded into the shape of the Star of David.

Even though this period was a time of great hope and triumph, it was also a time of tormented introspection. American Jews were still afflicted by the practical and philosophical struggles that emerged in the wake of the Holocaust. This tension was often expressed in synagogue art and architecture: emerging Jewish art of the 1950s and 1960s was particularly sorrowful, characterized as it was by twisted steel and contorted forms that clearly referred to the Jewish genocide.

Rough concrete and raw steel were often employed for synagogue buildings that, on the one hand, demonstrated man's triumph over these materials and, on the other, expressed a dark, somber sense of his powerlessness to achieve peace and harmony. Art historian Avram Kampf argues that the use of these 'primitive' materials reflects Jewish angst that God permitted the Holocaust to occur.[20] Max Abromovitz's Temple Beth Zion (1966) in Buffalo, New York, demonstrates this well. Its bold, concrete walls tilt out and project upwards, appearing to defy gravity. Inside, the sanctuary's soaring ark is both awesomely affirmative and solemnly humbling. It is a contemplative space that articulates the incomprehensible grief that engulfed the post-Holocaust Jewish world (*page 196*).

19 Frank Lloyd Wright, quoted in Roger G. Kennedy, *American Churches*, Crossroad, New York, 1982, p. 32.
20 Avram Kampf, *Contemporary Synagogue Art: Developments in the United States, 1945–1965*, Jewish Publication Society of America, Philadelphia, 1966, Chapter 1.

4 | CURRENT TRENDS

At the beginning of the twenty-first century, decades after the waves of Jewish
immigration to the United States have ended, synagogue design continues to evolve
in ways that reflect general changes in American society, as well as trends that are
specific to American Jewish life. In general, Jewish congregations are seeking new types
of spaces that respond more directly to their desire for community, intimacy, and
inclusiveness as parts of spiritual practice. Although other American religious groups
share many of these desires, Jews are engaged in a determined quest to define Jewish
traditions and create a sense of history that is authentic and meaningful. Today, that
search is being expressed in the design of contemporary American synagogues.

American Jews are no longer immigrants but full-fledged members of American
society who have become more willing to express their status as a unique religious
group; they are more forthright in building houses of worship that express their ethnic
identity. No longer seeking to build religious homes that blend with other ecclesiastical
buildings, Jewish congregations and their architects continue to look for architectural
solutions that reflect their unique ethnic roots and religious ideals. Rather than
looking to the Diaspora for cultural inspiration, many congregations are instead
exploring ways to draw closer to their universal Jewish roots in Israel.

The search for Jewish identity is especially pressing in contemporary American
society. The homogenization of material and cultural goods has created a spiritual void
that has slowed the dynamism of an otherwise diverse society. Modern means of
communication have brought Americans closer to people around the globe, and
yet these same technologies also curtail meaningful daily social interactions.

As a result, Jewish Americans—like many Americans—crave more from
community life. Congregations are beginning to offer even more comprehensive social

OPPOSITE: *Loggia, Gates of
the Grove Synagogue,
East Hampton, New York
(1989).*

functions, to create inviting environments, and to encourage people of all ages to participate in the social and religious life of their communities. Recently, the fear of terrorism on United States soil has further underscored the importance of group support in coping with life-changing events that are beyond a congregation's control. For American Jews this means a return to the synagogue and a need for changes in the American synagogue itself.

INCLUSIVE, DEMOCRATIC SPACE

In recent years, Jewish religious services have become more democratic, more personal, and less hierarchical than ever before. Often more educated about the Jewish liturgy than their parents, Jewish congregants want to participate actively in services, rather than remain mere spectators of the primary event. The differences between the clergy and laity are also being redefined, and men and women are gaining a more equal status in synagogue life. These shifts are emerging in architectural settings as congregations are changing the placement of arks, bimot, and seating in sanctuaries and chapels.

The most dramatic change in synagogue design is the reintroduction of traditional, communal-style seating. While new community spaces for socializing were incorporated into modern synagogues, many post-war Reform and Conservative synagogues still employed theater-style seating plans that prevented, rather than encouraged, interaction among worshippers as a group. Congregations seeking more intimate spaces are reorganizing sanctuary seating so that members have clear views of the reader as well as their fellow congregants as they pray, which in turn enhances the communal nature of the service. Some congregations that previously used theater-style seating have moved the bimah to the center of the sanctuary, so that the reading of the Torah can take place in the midst of the membership. By reinstating the central bimah plan, these congregations are readopting traditional seating. In some Orthodox synagogues, the second-level galleries have been eliminated in order to bring women [down to the main floor, and] closer to the services.

As a result, contemporary rituals are literally and metaphorically more accessible. In modern synagogues built in the decades following World War II, the bimah and ark were often raised high, creating a stage-like setting that was reserved for the clergy and select honored congregants. Now, the bimah and the ark are frequently lowered to bring them closer to the congregants, both physically and emotionally. In the new chapel at Congregation Rodeph Sholom in New York, the clergy sits among the congregants when they are not officiating, rather than above and apart.

In general, Jewish congregations are searching to renew their Jewish roots by participating in traditional rituals. Even Reform congregations are reaffirming traditions which their parents and grandparents had abandoned just decades before. The wearing of *kippot* and *talit*, the use of Hebrew rather than English in religious services, and the placement of the ark at the east-facing wall have all been revived recently by many Reform congregations.

SACRED SPACE, SPIRITUAL PLACE

Just as religious services are becoming more personal and intimate, the practice of Judaism, like other religions, is beginning to integrate new kinds of spirituality that recognize the beauty of nature and seek meditative tranquility. In the early twenty-first century, congregations are collaborating with architects to create meaningful designs that strengthen their Jewish identity through the use of truthful and expressive physical forms. They are achieving this goal by introducing new Jewish themes and treating them in non-traditional ways that go far beyond the use of historic symbols such as the menorah or the Star of David. Likewise, the tremendous increase in the production of Jewish art in the last 50 years indicates that American Jews are making a spirited effort to convey the Jewish experience in a much more contemporary way.

Although most religious services have traditionally taken place in large sanctuaries, many congregations now desire smaller settings for spiritual worship than they did in the past. Congregations that did not have small side chapels are now adding them to their synagogues; in many cases they are abandoning the main sanctuary for everything but major holidays. The newer spaces tend to be much smaller, more intimate, and more readily adaptable to group participation.

ABOVE: *Ark gates by Laurie Gross in the new rooftop chapel, Congregation Rodeph Sholom, New York, New York (2003).*

ABOVE: *Temple Beth Shalom,*
Hastings-on-Hudson,
New York (1999).

Increasingly, congregations are offering multiple services to accommodate diverse styles of observance desired by their members. As the need for multiple prayer settings becomes more widespread, these alternate services are affecting synagogue design.

Congregations are also forging increasingly close relationships with local communities and their surroundings at large. The term 'sanctuary' denotes a place of sanctity, but also a space of refuge from daily life. In the past, sanctuaries were often designed to eliminate visual contact with the outside world. Stained glass was used to allow light to enter the sanctuary while keeping the congregation's attention focused on the services within.

The interior spaces of many recent synagogues, on the other hand, incorporate the natural environment, or foreground views of the local scenery, or maximize the entry of natural light. Stained glass may still be used, but as a form of embellishment rather than as a means of secluding congregants from the outside world. One example is Temple De Hirsh Sinai (2001) in Bellevue, Washington, where clear glass spans the entire eastern wall of the sanctuary. In this way, nature becomes integrated directly into the spiritual experience (*page 232*).

The designs of many recent synagogues also reflect the architecture of the regions in which they are built. They represent a type of contextualism that has gained ground in American architecture in general. Temple Beth Shalom (1994) in Hastings-on-Hudson, New York, is a good example of a synagogue that blends in with its natural surroundings. Here, the synagogue conforms to the site's natural contours. The interior space is unadorned, tranquil, and open to the outdoors; abundant clear glass exposes the expanse of the sky and landscape.

These approaches indicate a perceptible break from the insular, impersonal modernism of earlier buildings like Frank Lloyd Wright's Temple Beth Shalom or Philip Johnson's Knesses Tifereth Israel. These new buildings embody a new attitude about the spatial character of a sanctuary as it relates to spiritual worship. The use of clear glass represents an openness that complements the return of the central bimah plan and the lowering of the ark, while nature is no longer considered to be a distraction from religious practice as it had been in the past.

The design of contemporary sanctuaries is also changing in other ways; most notably, in terms of their decoration and the use of Jewish art. And just as American synagogues are developing unique forms of Jewish expression, Jewish art is changing as well, becoming more cerebral, contemplative, and sophisticated than it has been in the past. While many congregations adorn their synagogues with Jewish objects and motifs, these traditional elements are being reinterpreted in ways that resonate more openly with modern lives.

Certainly, liturgical objects are one aspect of religious practice where creative, contemporary Jewish themes are starting to emerge, and they are changing the interior environment of synagogues. New traditional memorial markers or *yartzeit* plaques at the West End Synagogue in New York (1996) are one example (*page 70*). Traditionally, these inscribed plaques are fastened to a larger tablet connected to the wall, and an electric light bulb is illuminated next to each plaque on the anniversary of the honored one's death. At the West End Synagogue, a simple shelf is used in place of each bulb, and a black stone is placed on the shelf as a token of remembrance, in a ritual that recalls the Jewish commemorative practice of placing stones on a person's grave. This new interpretation of a traditional practice is not only more imaginative, but also gains strength by physically including mourners in the ritual of memorial.

Some architects have taken an artistic approach to Jewish iconography and inscriptions, at times inserting biblical quotes into the architecture itself. This includes the incorporation of spiritual and even mystical themes that are taken directly from the Torah. The ark in the Congregation Micah Synagogue (1997) in Nashville, Tennessee demonstrates this trend. Inspired by the phrase, 'it is a tree of life to them,' which refers to the Torah, the sanctuary is dominated by an ark in the form of a tree that grows from the floor (*page 214*). It is an abstract, rather than a literal form, that could also be interpreted as a menorah. At Larchmont Temple in Larchmont, New York, bronze rams' horns are integrated into the bimah; this reference comes directly from descriptions of the Tabernacle in the Book of Exodus.

ARCHITECTURE OF IDENTITY

As contemporary Jewish congregations seek to imbue their synagogues with spiritual meaning, they are finding inspiration in traditional Jewish forms. American congregations and their architects are seeking historical models from ancient Israel, as well as from the more recent Jewish past.

The reemergence of the wooden synagogue developed by Polish Jews—one of the most distinctive synagogue typologies in the history of the Diaspora—is perhaps the most palpable example of the kind of reinterpretation that is happening today. The image of the Polish synagogue has become a powerful and lasting symbol of Ashkenazi Americans' ancestry in Central Europe, and its use has not been limited to those congregations with Polish origins. A Reform congregation, Beth Shalom Rodef Zedek, built a new synagogue in Chester, Connecticut, that refers to the Polish synagogue in both plan and materials. In a new synagogue that was recently completed in Michigan for a school for Hasidim—a sect of Judaism that began in seventeenth-century Poland—the building's post-and-beam timber system makes a visible reference to the congregation's distant Polish roots (*page 252*). A synagogue for a Reconstructionist congregation in California was based on the wooden synagogue even though the traditions and climate of that state are quite different from Northern Europe.

Other congregations are reaching even further back historically, making reference to their biblical roots in the Holy Land. Whatever their views on Zionism or Israeli politics, American Jews continue to maintain strong emotional ties to Israel. For centuries, Jews prayed to move back to Jerusalem, but few had the chance to ever set foot in the city. Today, many have visited the Holy Land, and their journeys are touching them in indelible ways. The impact of these visits, and American Jews' increased connection to Israel in general, is emerging in the elements, materials, and spatial organizations of synagogues across the United States. Synagogue architects often emulate—however generally—the layout of Solomon's temple in ancient Jerusalem. In their designs, they incorporate certain Middle Eastern elements, such as Islamic archways and decoration derived from old Hebrew pattern books. Overt imitation of Middle Eastern ornament is rare, however, and the sophisticated and intricate decoration of the Moorish style that was once considered authentically Jewish is a thing of the past. Other American synagogues make references to the architecture of the modern Holy Land. San Antonio's Agudas Achim, inspired by modern Israeli architecture, combines simple, geometric forms organized around open courtyards. Middle Eastern details include arches and domes that are shaped from solid materials such as masonry and concrete, and a geometric, faceted roof.

The most common overt reference to Israel is the use of Jerusalem stone for flooring, wall surfaces, and exterior façades. A variety of limestone quarried near Jerusalem, it is mandatory for buildings constructed in the Holy City. Rather than use limestone quarried locally, many American congregations insist on importing Jerusalem stone from Israel, thus demonstrating their desire for authenticity and a connection to their roots. Its use recalls in particular the Jewish quarter of the Old City, where the Western Wall or 'Wailing Wall' is located. The stone's historical symbolism is most dramatic when it is used in the synagogue sanctuary as a backdrop to the ark, creating a more explicit suggestion of the Wailing Wall. These allusions to the Western Wall suggest congregations' continued desire to include iconic, authentically Jewish forms in the synagogue.

Contemporary congregations have encouraged the frequent use of Hebrew quotes and phrases on building façades, in artwork, and on sanctuary walls, even in those synagogues where the use of English predominated a generation ago. In many ways, the Hebrew characters are a visual representation of Judaism at its most elemental—it is the written language of those who proudly call themselves 'the People of the Book.'

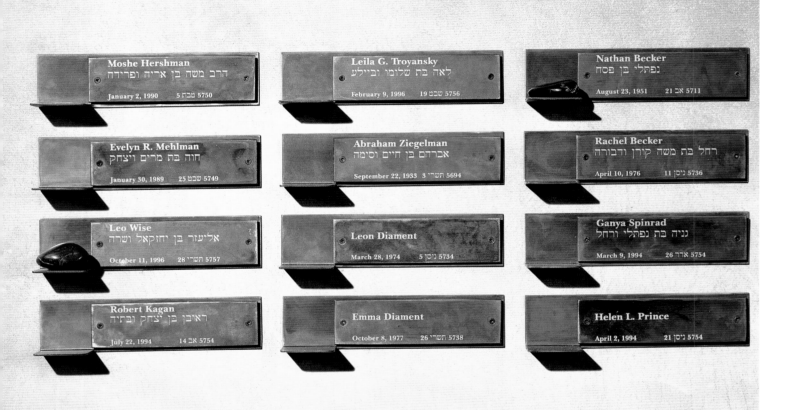

Moshe Hershman
הרב משה בן אריה ופרידה
January 2, 1990   5 שבט 5750

Leila G. Troyansky
לאה בת שלומו ובײלע
February 9, 1996   19 שבט 5756

Nathan Becker
נפתלי בן פסח
August 23, 1951   21 אב 5711

Evelyn R. Mehlman
חוה בת מרים ויצחק
January 30, 1989   25 שבט 5749

Abraham Ziegelman
אברהם בן חיים וסימה
September 22, 1933   3 תשרי 5694

Rachel Becker
רחל בת משה קורן ודבורה
April 10, 1976   11 ניסן 5736

Leo Wise
אליעזר בן יחזקאל ושרה
October 11, 1996   28 תשרי 5757

Leon Diament
March 28, 1974   5 ניסן 5734

Ganya Spinrad
גניה בת נפתלי ורחל
March 9, 1994   26 אדר 5754

Robert Kagan
ראובן בן יצחק ובתיה
July 22, 1994   14 אב 5754

Emma Diament
October 8, 1977   26 תשרי 5738

Helen L. Prince
April 2, 1994   21 ניסן 5754

After almost three centuries of synagogue architecture in America, we can see that American synagogues are the expression of two simultaneous evolutions.

The first is that of American architecture. Synagogues readily adopted American design trends, so much so that they sometimes resemble other, non-Jewish religious buildings built during the same period. For many congregations, the use of the latest architectural fashion was a proud symbol of Jews' integration into society.

American Jewry itself has undergone profound transformations—both social and religious—over the course of its history. American synagogues bear witness to this second evolutionary process: the adoption of new values, new ways of life, and new religious practices.

For first-generation Jewish immigrants who came to America in search of a better life, prominent synagogues were symbols of their communities' success in mainstream American society. Later, when American Jews re-evaluated the role of the synagogue in Jewish life, synagogues became community centers as well as houses of worship.

As we look towards the future, we can expect that synagogue design will continue to follow the same paths. Synagogues will continue to evolve along with the identity of the American Jewish community, while maintaining the architectural language of American design. Smaller, community-oriented spaces, for example, have emerged as Jews seek a more intimate interpretation of Jewish worship and community. The role of synagogues is also expanding as Jews participate to a far greater extent in the cultural and social lives of their congregations.

The synagogue—like architectural fashions and religious identity—is a malleable concept that is constantly open to change. Yet the synagogue's centrality in American Jewish life has never wavered. In fact, in today's complex times, the synagogue will likely be more central than ever before. In the United States, where Jews' lives are relatively integrated within secular society, the synagogue must remain a lasting, significant institution if it is to ensure the continuity of the Jewish community in the years to come. To realize that goal, American Jews must imagine a synagogue architecture that fosters community while expressing their shared Jewish identity in a meaningful way. Only then will they create a place of celebration and spirituality, people-hood and prayer that is relevant to modern Jewish life.

OPPOSITE: *Memorial plaques by Douglas Riccardi, West End Synagogue (1996). These Yartzeit plaques interpret an old tradition of putting rocks on graves to honor a person's death. Instead of memorial lights, small stones placed on a shelf invoke the commemorative ritual.*

SYNAGOGUES AND AMERICAN SPIRITUALITY

RABBI LAWRENCE A. HOFFMAN

BARBARA & STEPHEN FRIEDMAN PROFESSOR OF LITURGY WORSHIP & RITUAL

HEBREW UNION COLLEGE, NEW YORK

Though concern with spirituality is ancient, its mantra-like use to imply religious 'authenticity' is quintessentially contemporary and American. Synagogues as spiritual places, therefore, is a novel—and even suspicious—notion, especially for Jews, who may know that there is no traditional Hebrew equivalent for 'spiritual,' and who (if born before World War II) are likely to wonder what 'spiritual' even is. Its novelty, however, does not necessarily disqualify it as an apt description of what Jews have sought before, albeit in different guises, and known by other names.

The current fascination with spirituality should be traced to aging baby-boomers, people born between 1946 and 1964. They grew up surrounded by the new-age religious din of the 1960s and '70s, and are described (most famously, perhaps) as a generation of spiritual seekers, raised with a sense of entitlement to their own expressive individualism.[1] Since the boomer generation is the largest cohort ever to have been born in this country, the odds are that if you are reading this book, the boomers are you.

If you are a Jew in the older boomer crowd (in your fifties by now) you were indelibly touched by the Vietnam War, and remember student 'radicals' who shut down universities. You may have been (or wanted to be) a 'hippie,' enjoyed (or wanted to enjoy) the sexual revolution, and slogged through (or wish you had slogged through) the mud at Woodstock. Your pre-war suburban parents have been likened to a generation who raised you in 'corporate suburban synagogues,' emphasizing 'uniform behavior and uniform prayer'—all of which your generation rejected.[2] If you are the

OPPOSITE: *Stained glass windows, North Shore Hebrew Academy, Kings Point, New York (1999). The composition represents the kabbalistic creation myth known as 'the breaking of the vessels.'*

1 Cf. Wade Clark Roof, *A Generation of Seekers,* Harper Collins, New York, 1993; Robert N. Bellah et. al., *Habits of the Heart,* Harper and Rowe, New York, 1985.

2 Riv-Ellen Prell, *Prayer and Community,* Wayne State, Detroit, 1989, p. 31.

second wave of boomers (now in your forties), you became a teen after Vietnam, watched a shift in population and power to the sunbelt, and saw a conservative reaction blanket the country. Either way, the newfound word 'spirituality' infiltrated your consciousness via television, movies, and mega-bookstores. For the earlier wave of boomers, the religio-cultural landmarks were the plethora of alternative religions founded in the late 1960s and early '70s (Krishna consciousness in 1965; transcendental meditation in 1966, the Divine Light Mission in 1971); for the younger boomers, it was born-again Christianity initiated with Key '73 but mainstreamed in the Reagan years of 1980–1988.

In both cases, spirituality was set against what the boomers saw as lifeless religious institutionalism. That distinction was hardly new to America: it is central to the Transcendentalism of Ralph Waldo Emerson (1803–1882) and is a philosophical basis for the 1901–02 lectures by William James, which he published famously as *The Varieties of Religious Experience*. But only the baby-boomers, seeking personal growth, inner discovery, and religious intimacy, read magazines that began with *People*, moved on to *Us* and culminated in *Self*.[3] Protestant Christianity, once typified by claims of human moral depravity, transformed traditional rhetoric of fire and brimstone into promises of love, solace, and help with various addictions—substance abuse, bad marriages, worldly ambition and the workplace. Jews too now personalize worship and attend services of healing.

Spirituality was plotted more than it was found; invented rather than discovered, by rabbis and pastors who hoped it would offset such things as Hare Krishna, EST, new-age Buddhism, and plain religious 'dropoutism.' It was the religious dimension of the massive shift in consciousness toward looking deep within the 'self,' and daring to go public about what one found there: alcoholism, co-dependency, victimization as a child, poor or abandoned marriages, depression, overeating, and a host of other maladies that medicine could not cure but spirituality might address. But it was more than twelve-step programs going mainstream. A seismic rumbling shook up established religion with a spiritual invasion of meditation and mantras, ecological consciousness, popularizations of spiritual classics, and a fetish for 'meaningful' relationships. This is spirituality driven by the self and for the self. It is largely non-institutional. It is just peaking and has a way to go. It is the very opposite of the kind of religion envisioned by suburban synagogues. It is just now being reflected in synagogue architecture.

The question is whether spirituality was really, as the boomers charged, absent from prior synagogue architecture or whether other forms of spirituality have dominated synagogue design, even if the word 'spirituality' was not applied to them.

3   George Gallup, Jr. and Timothy Jones, *The Next American Spirituality: Finding God in the Twenty-First Century,* Victor Cook Communications, Colorado Springs, 2000, p. 50.

Synagogues arose around the turn of the common era—but certainly not (as is often claimed) as a response to the destruction of the Solomonic Temple and the ensuing Babylonian exile of 587 B.C.E. But the false notion that synagogues arose to replace the first Temple is worth looking at, if only to uncover the latent myth behind it. It assumes that the synagogue was originally a place of Jewish worship, as the Temple had been. Nothing could be farther from the truth. Not only did the synagogue not develop in 587, but even when it did come into being, it was not intended as a place of prayer. The earliest pre-70 C.E. synagogue buildings so far unearthed have been aptly described as 'neutral communal structures with no notable religious components— neither inscriptions, artistic representations, nor the presence of a Torah shrine. The first-century synagogue did not have the decidedly religious profile that it was to acquire by late antiquity.'[4]

Spirituality of some sort there may have been, but not through worship, and not, therefore, in anything like the sanctuaries typical of synagogues pictured in this book. The first synagogues had varying floor plans. If they had arks at all, they were moveable until the third century or so, when permanent niches were carved into the wall facing Jerusalem, necessitating (in some cases) opening new entrances in the opposite wall, and closing up existing ones to make room for the niche. Only in the third century did synagogues finally proliferate, by then as places of prayer, and designed to face Jerusalem. Synagogues had become not just places of assembly, as the Greek word *synagoge*, and the parallel Hebrew *bet knesset* implies; and not just places of study (*bet midrash*); but places of prayer (*bet t'fillah*) as well.

They were, in fact, to different degrees in different eras, places of almost everything. For most of Jewish history, Jews were not citizens of a state and had no conception of religion—let alone of a building that was 'religious.' They were corporate members of a discrete group whose boundaries, rights and status were defined by their host societies, and whose address was the synagogue where they gathered for any number of reasons. In Renaissance Italy, for instance, the synagogue housed the Jewish court that ruled on questions of civil law. If people came to services, it was not necessarily for worship alone; it might equally have been to find out who was suing who. Even during the prayer service itself, a long-standing tradition allowed congregants to seek justice by interrupting services to announce grievances. Synagogues also had libraries, containing not just the Talmud and related literature, but in one case at least, even a translation of Aristotle.[5] So even after religion pervaded it, the synagogue remained much more than a religious institution alone.

Only when modernity redefined Judaism as a religion, did the synagogue become a center for what we consider the life of the spirit. In the age of growing nationalism, Jews could hardly remain a nation within a nation. Yearning for citizenship and the rights that went with it, European Jews declared themselves a religion, without yet even knowing fully what that was—which is not to say that premodern Jews were secular or areligious, but only that becoming modern, even modern Orthodox,

4 Lee I. Levine, *The Ancient Synagogue,* Yale University Press, New Haven, 2000, p. 70.
5 Robert Bonfil, *Rabbis and Jewish Communities in Renaissance Italy,* Oxford University Press, Oxford, 1990, pp. 178–179, 245, 276.

entailed a shift in consciousness by which religion was simply one category of many in one's identity, rather than 'a sacred canopy'[6] that covers every aspect of life in a taken-for-granted way. Religion was something you now chose to be (or to leave); and as much as it may have retained its hold on private and (for some) even communal life, it was no longer coterminous with the totality of Jewish life as it had been when Jews had been a separate corporate entity excluded from full membership in the modern nation state.

Modern Jews had necessarily to conceptualize religion as opposed to, say, the government, the modern justice system, or universities, which used to be institutions imposed on them or withheld from them, but were now theirs as well their neighbors'. Social life became fragmented into competing institutions that have been called 'finite provinces of meaning, enclaves of paramount reality' among which modern citizens commuted for different parts of their life experience.[7] As the church was the religious (but only the religious) center for Christians, the synagogue became the religious (but only the religious) center for Jews. Religion was not easily distinguished from ethnicity, however, and Jews defined 'religious' more broadly—it included *lernen* ('learning') as not just study but 'intrinsically religious activity' for instance.[8] But nonetheless, in a modern context, Jewish religious institutions were formulated like their Christian parallels.

For Christians, worship was religion's essence; and worship space the focus of the church, even of ethnic churches, founded as much to retain the 'old way of life,' religion and all, as just the religion alone. So modern synagogues too, even if similarly ethnic in their original appeal, became mostly places of worship, and the sanctuary their architectural center.

SYNAGOGUES AS SPIRITUAL PLACES

Assuming the western definition of religion as worship-centered, and recognizing different styles of Jewish worship throughout American history, we can stretch our concept of spirituality beyond the baby-boom variety, and see it as a potential quality of worship in general. We can then chart the history of North American synagogues as a creative interchange between the changing styles of prayer and the architecture designed to support them.

Before launching our survey, however, a vital corrective is in order. What normally gets discussed are the extraordinary examples of any given style, the architectural ideal types, as it were. These are the regularly photographed giants of their genre, designed by artistic masters of their time. It is arguable that spirituality can be found in any one of them, simply by virtue of the genius of their artistry. But most American Jews of any period do not worship in these structures. They are limited to less expensive versions of whatever the dominant style is. In the suburban era, for instance, we will have occasion to see the stunning treatments of the bimah space by Percival Goodman, who accommodated suburban priorities of school wings and

6   A classical conception by now: see Peter Berger, *The Sacred Canopy*, Anchor Books, New York, 1969.

7   Peter L. Berger and Thomas Luckmann, *The Social Construction of Reality*, New York, 1967, p. 25. The process of enclave formation has continued apace, and is seen now in terms of spirituality (Robert N. Bellah, et. al., *Habits of the Heart*, New York, 1985, pp. 171–175); and in emerging studies of Gen X, people born between 1961 and 1981 (or after 1964, according to some). Cf. Richard R. Flory and Donald E. Miller, *GenX Religion*, New York, 2000; Jackson W. Carroll and Wade Clark Roof, *Bridging Divided Worlds*, San Francisco, 2002.

8   Samuel Heilman, *The People of the Book*, Chicago, 1983, p. 242.

expansion space without sacrificing the sanctuary area. Less talented designers bowed to the conventions of their time without successfully spiritualizing the shrinking sanctuary space at all—the ubiquitous longitudinal pews facing up to a stage-box bimah, for example. If we find, therefore, that synagogues have always supported spiritual worship of one kind or another, we should remember that our samples are usually just the best of an era. With that caveat in mind, we can turn to the synagogues, organized (as in this book) according to immigration waves, and ask how features of their design responded to the modern Jew's quest for a synagogue as a place of public prayer.

During the first wave of Jewish immigration here, Ashkenazi Jews (Jews from Central Europe) quickly predominated, but it began with Sephardim—Jews who trace their roots to the Iberian peninsula, and then, by way of Holland, to Dutch colonies in South America, and finally to New Amsterdam (later New York).

Sephardi synagogues include New York's Shearith Israel (1730) and Touro Synagogue in Newport, Rhode Island (1762), but we know relatively little about the actual worship there. Of the original Shearith Israel building on Mill Street, we have only pictures,[9] and the Touro synagogue (*page 96*) was not constructed until 1762, a little over a century after its community was founded (1658). Our best guess at what the first Sephardi synagogue here looked like comes from a synagogue in Curacao, which was enlarged or rebuilt in 1733, but without destroying the initial structure of 1692. Its interior follows the standard Sephardi longitudinal seating plan (*page 29*). Still, the interior of the Touro synagogue does not, so some Sephardi synagogues, at least later, did not, in part (perhaps) because their architects followed paradigms from England which had been influenced by the Wren school of city church construction, rather than the closest Sephardi paradigm in Amsterdam.[10]

In any case, we do not know much about early American Sephardi worship. To be sure, Joseph Pinto, the eighteenth-century chazzan at Shearith Israel describes it as following the service of Amsterdam and England, but did it really? And did it everywhere? Can we trust the description of services given by the man charged with leading them?[11] Was there no syncretism at all between Sephardim and Ashkenazim— who were in the majority by the mid-eighteenth century, even though they prayed in Sephardi synagogues? We have too little information to know just what the Sephardi worship was like, how many people attended regularly, and what kind of spirituality it featured. We should assume some unique form of spirituality, however. Spanish Jews arrived with a considerable cultural repertoire of worship which American mores would have supported. Their synagogue came hand-in-hand with age-old customs rightly claimed as a unique Sephardi contribution to the spiritual life of the colonies.

9   Rachel Wischnitzer, *Synagogue Architecture,* Jewish Publication Society, Philadelphia, 1955, p. 11.

10 The Bevis Marks Synagogue of 1701. See Nancy Halverson Schless, 'Peter Harrison, The Touro Synagogue, and the Wren City Church,' *Winterthur Portfolio* 8, 1973, pp. 187–200. But cf. Wischnitzer, *Synagogue Architecture*, p. 11. For the great Portuguese synagogue of Amsterdam, see H.A. Meek, *The Synagogue*, Phaidon Press, London, 1995, pp. 136, 141. For Bevis Marks, see pp. 142–147; Touro is discussed on pp. 147–149, but without full view of interior.

11 De Sola Pool, *An Old Faith in a New World*, Chapter 4, describes worship, but most of the description is an anachronistic reading back from De Sola Pool's day.

We know more about nineteenth-century Jews of Central Europe, who swelled Jewish numbers here as the second wave of Jewish immigrants. Jewish population on the eve of the American revolution was less than 2000,[12] and by 1818, it had grown by only a thousand. But from 1818 to 1848, Jews from Germany (but also from Bohemia and what is now western Poland) expanded it to 50,000, and from 1848 to 1878, they enlarged it to 230,000, this time with a handful (but only a handful) of arrivals from what we consider eastern Europe (Russia, Romania, the Ukraine, and the like), where vast emigration did not begin in earnest until 1881.[13] In Germany, being a Jew usually meant automatically belonging to the Jewish community and its official residence, the synagogue. Here in America, these Jews were free to erect as many synagogues as they wanted.

And they built them specifically as places of worship. Protestantism, generally, and German Lutheranism in particular, viewed worship as the primary measuring rod of religiosity. So Ashkenazi synagogues limited themselves largely to worship. 'In most cases congregations did indeed maintain cemeteries, and, in a few, day schools, but that was the extent of it.'[14] Soon even cemetery servicing ceased, as professional funeral homes took their place. The result was a new kind of synagogue: not a statement of integral Jewish community, but a focus for religion, which was 'essentially confined to worship services.'[15]

Ashkenazi religion (for the Jewish upper class, anyway) was dependent on a philosophic view of worship newly circulating among German intellectuals.[16] Medieval thinkers (Jewish and Christian) had seen prayer as an obligation demanded by God; it would please God, who would respond positively to it. By the nineteenth century, however, philosophers were rejecting the idea of a personal God who simply 'liked' prayer. So prayer was for our sake, not God's. Its purpose was to instill inner devotion and moral enlightenment. Synagogues (like churches) were newly called 'God's House' (*Gotteshaus*), a place designed to impart reverence for the sacred and respect for the moral. Architects designed them with façades that set them apart from their secular urban surroundings, and outfitted them internally with dominating sanctuaries where worship would make the spirituality of 'God's House' patent.

Enlightened German Jews who arrived in America sought such a building, albeit filtered through uniquely American reasoning. In Europe, a community's synagogue had often been a Jewish community's official Jewish address. America's principle of religious freedom made that concept obsolete. But America had been founded on truly religious principles, and Jews who came here were expected to demonstrate some kind of authentic religious commitment. The economic boom following the civil war raised expectations to the point where, 'in the 1960s, there was hardly a congregation in America which did not build a large and sumptuous new edifice.'[17] These buildings took on special significance after 1881, when eastern European Jews, who knew nothing of central European high aesthetics, had begun to arrive in astounding numbers. The 230,000 American Jews of 1880 became 1,000,000

12   Joseph Leiser, *American Judaism: A Historical Survey*, Bloch, New York, 1925, p. 83.

13   Alan Silverstein, *Alternatives to Assimilation: The Response of Reform Judaism to American Culture*, Beacon Press, Hanover, 1994, p. 11.

14   Leon Jick, *The Americanization of the Synagogue, 1820-1870*, Hanover, NH, 1976, p. 30.

15   Daniel J. Elazar, 'The Development of the American Synagogue,' *Modern Judaism* 4:3, October 1984, p. 259.

16   For what follows, see Michael A. Meyer, '"How Awesome is This Place!" The Reconceptualization of the Synagogue in Nineteenth-Century Germany,' *Leo Baeck Yearbook 41*, 1996, pp. 51–63.

17   Jick, *Americanization*, p. 179.

in 1900, 3,500,000 in 1915, and 4,500,000 by 1925, the year after immigration was cut off.[18] The need to differentiate themselves from their poor eastern cousins produced what we call 'classical Reform Judaism,' a unique style of prayer designed to promote a distinctly awesome sense of the sacred. Here was a new kind of spirituality in which space, text and choreography colluded.

This European sense of the holy, common to many Christians as well as Jews, was best expressed by Rudolph Otto, whose landmark book, *The Idea of the Holy* is still required reading for many religion undergraduates. For Otto, the holy is synonymous with the sense of awe. God is the numinous reality beyond all description, a distant and transcendent deity before whom we humans become instantly silenced by the recognition of our own paltry finitude. It is tempting to see this doctrine as a projection of Otto's own upbringing. He was raised according to 'enlightened' German child-rearing theory that urged mothers to teach their children self-discipline by keeping their distance to the point of ignoring them—a childhood he mirrored as an adult by remaining an aloof professor whom students actually called 'Der Heilige,' the 'Holy One.'[19] But both Otto and the religious style he described are hardly idiosyncratic. They symbolize a larger German cultural complex, Otto being the ideal type to which religious souls aspired, and 'sacred otherness' being the cultural ideal that attracted them.

This image was so thoroughly embedded in mainline American culture, that to this day we take it for granted as universal, rather than see it as the culturally contingent concept that it is. German Jews brought it here with magnificent cathedral synagogues that exemplified an inherent chasm between the transcendent holy God and ordinary mortal worshipers.

Temple Emanu-El of New York (*page 162*), built in 1929, is perhaps the finest example.[20] Its two massive external doors protect the sacred interior from the profane din of ordinary life. As one passes through the doors, one leaves the everyday world behind. The foyer immediately inside is tiny, since the synagogue is not a place to meet and greet. Talk ceases there. The sacred is a serious matter, inviting human communion with the divine alone.

From the tiny foyer, one moves immediately, and quietly, into the sanctuary. Looking straight ahead, one is struck by a magnificent cathedral-like space where a large frontal bimah is set high above the congregation, and provided with a side door through which the clergy can make entrances and exits without mixing with the crowd. Space is massive; ceilings high; architectural lines lead the gaze up and beyond, to a transcendent far-off deity. From some invisible point beyond the bimah, a disembodied choir delivers sophisticated music to passive worshipers in pews below, their personal identities submerged in a massive whole called the congregation.

A recent study shows Emanu-El's congregants still honoring the commanding silence of the sanctuary setting by sitting with their immediate family members, but separate from other families already gathered. The discrete space between small family

18 Lloyd P. Gartner, 'Jewish Education in the United States,' in Marshall Sklare, ed., *The Jewish Community in America*, Behrman House, New York, 1974, p. 232.

19 Donald Capps, *Men Religion and Melancholy: James, Otto, Jung and Erikson*, Yale University Press, New Haven, 1997, pp. 76–126.

20 See also, Oscar Israelowitz, *Synagogues of New York City: A Pictorial Survey*, Dover Press, New York, 1982, which includes rarely accessible synagogues outside of Manhattan.

groups discourages interpersonal discourse and encourages meditation with the divine.[21] The service proceeds with dignified solemnity underscored by the choir's sacred sound, the reader's mellifluous prose, the high register of the English prayers, and the architectural magnificence. The sanctuary is so central that space for events other than worship is tucked away in the basement or upper floors, hard even to get to from the main entrance that announces the real purpose of the structure: the soul's communion with God in God's house.

Communion with God has also saturated the prayer experience of many Orthodox Jews who have frequented storefront *minyanim* (prayer gatherings), or synagogues that were not part of the grandeur and dignity of Cathedral Judaism. Traditionally Orthodox Jews still tend toward a relationship with a personal God active in the universe and in individual lives,[22] and that attitude is hardly new, so I do not mean to limit spirituality to the kind of reverential worship that Otto described. (At the end of this essay, I will return to the spirituality of personal piety that demands no building at all.) But modernity has always beckoned Jews to move in the direction of grand aesthetics. Witness the 1861 Forsyth Street congregation in New York which was split apart by Hasidic 'dissidents' who are described at the time as being 'on intimate terms with the Almighty...abhor[ing] decorum...[and] scorn[ing] a regularly ordained cantor whom they are not allowed and cannot follow in his 'foreign' melodies.'[23] So for now, our story is dependent on the Central European adulation of monumental space, magnificent music, and a transcendent deity—a combination that was only enhanced by the financial windfall in the 1860s and continued until World War II.

Temple Emanu-El of New York highlighted that cathedral-synagogue style. It survives, relatively unchanged—a reminder of an era that came to an end by the 1950s.

POST-WAR SUBURBIA

Until the 1950s, in large German-Jewish synagogues like Emanu-El, but also in smaller ones in the American hinterland, worship was primary. Childhood education, though important, was relegated to cramped quarters abutting the sanctuary or the sanctuary itself when prayer was not in session. In the 1950s, however, the relative importance of these two functions was reversed: services were marginalized, while childhood education took precedence. Eventually, 'synagogues began to provide school wings for Sunday schools and occasional afternoon Hebrew schools. Adult needs were met with large social halls and catering facilities.' That left 'a sanctuary of moderate size, that because of economic necessity, needs to expand into another area, (usually the social hall) for the High Holidays...We also have administrative facilities, gift shops, board rooms, youth lounges, and on rare occasions, a *mikveh* (ritual bath).'[24]

In March of 1947, already seeing this reversal in priorities, *Commentary* (then the primary Jewish journal for elite readers) invited the former curator of the Jewish Museum in Berlin, Rachel Wischnitzer-Bernstein to discuss 'The Problem of Synagogue Architecture.' The following June, her article was followed by a symposium that

21 Angela Warner Buchdahl, *Music and Identity at Temple Emanu-El, B'nai Jeshurun, and Chavurat Tikvah,* unpublished cantorial masters thesis, Hebrew Union College–Jewish Institute of Religion, New York, 1999.

22 Samuel C. Heilman and Steven M. Cohen, *Cosmopolitans and Parochials,* Chicago, 1989, pp. 90–94.

23 J. D. Eisenstein, 'The History of the First Russian-American Jewish Congregation,' *Publications of the American Jewish Historical Society* 9, 1901, p. 68.

24 Benjamin Hirsch, 'Synagogue Roles and Design,' *New Conversations* 5:2, Fall 1980, p. 2.

brought together art historian Fritz Landsberger and three outstanding synagogue architects: Ely Kahn, Percival Goodman, and Eric Mendelsohn.[25] Goodman collaborated on his remarks with his brother Paul, who was emerging as a literary critic and ideologue of the new left.

The *Commentary* dialogue fastened on the need for an architectural style distinctive to American Judaism come of age. Wischnitzer had emphasized the nineteenth-century European tendency to lend synagogues the weight of tradition by linking them to historical eras of Jewish life, usually by way of an Egyptian or Moorish design, on the grounds that Judaism had arisen and flourished as an 'Oriental' phenomenon. The Moorish pattern continued in America, as did other romanticizations reaching back to a halcyon past—the neo-classicism of New York's Shearith Israel, for instance (*page 132*). But Wischnitzer trashed history as a model for her own present, especially after World War II, whose 'bitter lessons mean a respect for the small, intimate and humble things, for what is unpretentious and human in scale.'[26]

The sub-titles supplied by the participants in the follow-up dialogue show just how much their authors agreed with Wischnitzer's encouragement to shake off European prototypes: Kahn calls his contribution, 'No More Copying,' Mendelsohn addresses 'The Spirit of our Age', the Goodmans proclaim 'tradition from function.'[27] But architecture wasn't in crisis so much as Judaism was. It wasn't just the war; it was the post-war generation for whom cathedral-like spirituality was obsolete.

Truth be told, it is not entirely clear how well the old cathedral tradition had worked in America anyway. Grand synagogues had become places to see and be seen, not just for German Jews, but for upwardly bound eastern European Jews too, at the Eldridge Street Synagogue (*page 122*) where, at the height of immigration to the Lower East Side, the wealthy came weekly to enjoy the status of praying with the great cantor Pinchas Minkowsky.[28] Showpiece Conservative synagogues before the war—to which acculturated eastern European Jews were attracted—also featured 'cathedralism' with the traditionalism of cantors and choirs.

Those were the showcases, however, and most Conservative synagogues were not showcases. Conservatism was almost entirely eastern European, and children of eastern European immigrants who reached adulthood only in the depression years lacked financial means to design magnificent structures. Pre-war Conservative (and Orthodox) synagogues were sometimes the grand sort of thing that we see in older Reform Temples or even in the Orthodox Eldridge Street synagogue built for the first-generation eastern-European wealthy. But most were not.

Services had changed too. To begin with, even Reform worship had attracted mostly women,[29] whom Victorian culture had relegated to the home where they were charged with inculcating proper moral conduct in their children. Synagogue sanctuaries were just that, 'sanctuaries,' where women and children congregated as 'protected species' far from the cutthroat world of business. Conservative Jews, meanwhile, were 'for the greater part of the twentieth century' virtually

25 Rachel Wischnitzer-Bernstein, 'The Problem of Synagogue Architecture: Creating a Style Expressive of America,' *Commentary*, March, 1947, pp. 233–241; Franz Landsberger, Ely Jacque Kahn, Eric Mendelsohn, Percival and Paul Goodman, 'Creating a Modern Synagogue Style' A Discussion, *Commentary*, June, 1947, pp. 537–544.

26 Wischnitzer-Bernstein, p. 241.

27 But see Percival and Paul Goodman, 'Modern Artist as Synagogue Builder,' *Commentary* 7, Jan 1949, pp. 51–55, where the authors recognize that determining function is no easy matter. 'The very act of analyzing function and expressing meaning makes the artists soon turn on their employers with persistent embarrassing questions and paradoxes; they point out inconsistencies in the program' (p. 54). Post-war Jews claimed to know what they wanted (childhood education, for instance) but were unwilling to put the full force of their check-book and their will behind it.

28 Jeffrey S. Gurock, 'A Stage in the Emergence of the Americanized Synagogue Among East European Jews: 1890–1910,' *Journal of American Ethnic History* 9:2, 1990, pp. 7–25.

29 Synagogue services in general were 'peopled principally by women' (Alexandra Shecket Korros and Jonathan D. Sarna, *American Synagogue History: A Bibliography and State-Of-The-Field Survey*, Marcus Wiener, New York, 1988, p. 8.) The same was true of churches. In the suburban 1950s, Hartford's First Church was surprised to find that 50 percent of its Sunday congregants were male, a 'very unusual circumstance' (Robert S. Ellwood, *1950: Crossroads of American Religious Life*, Westminster John Knox Press, Louisville, 2000, p. 109.)

indistinguishable from those claiming to be Orthodox,[30] in that even though their worship style remained traditional, and even though many still attended when they could, the majority of neither camp could be called dedicated religionists intent on serious Sabbath prayer. There were exceptions, of course, but for many, if they went at all, it was out of old-world habit, 'nostalgia,'[31] or for ethnic camaraderie. Most, moreover, had to work Saturday mornings—in Wilkes-Barre, Pennsylvania, for instance, out of 250 families, only some half-dozen attended Shabbat morning services.[32] Both Conservative and (at one time) Orthodox Jews, like Reform, introduced late Friday night prayer, when men might choose to attend.[33]

But eastern European Jews had not been indoctrinated with Otto's notion of the holy, and America was increasingly becoming eastern European. Less and less did people attend for an experience of a transcendent deity. The cathedral synagogue spoke eloquently of Jewish 'arrival': its interior was awe-inspiring. But fewer and fewer Jews wanted spiritual inspiration, except on the High Holidays, perhaps. The very designation 'high' says it all. The traditional term, *yamim nora'im*, translates best as 'days of fright,' or (if that is too frightening), 'days of awe.' The new word 'high' mirrored the architectural and theological idiom of high ceilings, 'high church' worship, and a God on high, which was becoming increasingly irrelevant anyway, even in Protestantism, where Episcopalian worship was losing ground to the populism of Methodists and Baptists.

Other than the High Holy Days, the cathedral synagogue was a museum in the making. With European models particularly irrelevant after the war, Jews headed for the suburbs where synagogues would function quite differently.[34]

SUBURBAN RELIGION

More than a spiritual practice, suburban religion was America's symbolic statement of its fight against Godless communism. As Americans staked out the suburban frontier, churches and synagogues went up like gasoline stations on every corner. But how different they were from their cathedral-like urban predecessors.

A case in point is Temple Mishkan Tefila. It had been established in Boston's downtown Roxbury section, in 1858.[35] By 1910, the original German-born families had acculturated, and had been joined by Jews from Austria, Hungary and points farther east. Finding itself equally uncomfortable with purely Germanic Reform and with old-country Orthodoxy, the synagogue elected as rabbi Herman H. Rubenovitz, a member of the first graduating class of Conservative Judaism's Jewish Theological Seminary. Rubenovitz spoke for his congregants when he situated his congregation somewhere between Reform 'Temple Jews' who suffered 'assimilation running ragged,' and Orthodox 'Shul Jews,' plagued by 'immobility and stagnation.'[36]

Not being German himself, Rubenovitz had chosen Conservative over Reform. He favored traditionalism and even attended the 1913 Zionist Council in Basle (anathema to German Jews who considered Zionism anti-American). Until then, he

30 Jeffrey Gurock, David W. Belin Lecture in American Jewish Affairs, 7, *From Fluidity to Rigidity: The Religious Worlds of Conservative and Orthodox Jews in Twentieth Century America*, University of Michigan, Ann Arbor, 1998, p. 5.

31 Ibid., p. 33.

32 Ibid., p. 9.

33 Ibid., p. 27.

34 On which, see esp., Lance J. Sussman, 'The Suburbanization of American Judaism as Reflected in Synagogue Building and Architecture, 1945–1975,' *American Jewish History* 75, 1985, 31–47.

35 The following is taken from Herbert J. Selib, ed., *Temple Mishkan Tefila - a History, 1858-1958*, H.M. Teich, Inc., Brookline, 1958.

36 Ibid., p. 19.

had mostly dedicated himself to remodeling Jewish education, to offset what he saw as the steady erosion of Jewish culture. But while attending the Zionist Council he visited synagogues in Paris, Berlin and Vienna, where, 'for the first time in my life I realized the inherent beauty and majesty in our traditional synagogue service when clothed in dignity, decorum, and glorious musical setting.'[37]

This eastern European Jew had encountered western European Judaism, and as a result, returned to Boston less interested in education than in worship. Almost immediately he fought and won the right to install an organ and add a mixed choir to services. Then, in 1922, he personally broke ground for a new synagogue that would highlight the glorious experience of prayer that he had witnessed in Europe. His altered agenda, from education to prayer, can be seen in the stages of his synagogue's coming into being. The sanctuary was completed in 1925; only in 1929 did the school building become a reality.

The downtown synagogue revolved about its magnificent sanctuary of 1650 seats. It featured a late Friday night service, with a renowned cantor, organist and choir. According to Israel J. Kazis, Rubenovitz's rabbinic successor, until at least 1953 it attracted no fewer than 1000 worshipers every Friday night, and was sometimes filled to capacity. There is some reason to believe that Kazis overstated attendance.[38] Here especially, Kazis tells us that in 1956, the total membership was 692 families. If we make a conservative allowance for a quarter of the families being single (elderly widows, usually) and if we exclude children who would not have attended Friday night services, we find a total adult population of 1038. Nearly all of them would have had to come for Rabbi Kazis' average to be correct, still, even for the irreligious, Mishkan Tefila offered musical and sermonic substance, as well as after-service camaraderie. In an age when television was still coming into being, Friday night was still synagogue night for many, and before the rush to the suburbs, men worked just minutes away from home, so had time to eat Shabbat dinner and go to Temple.

By 1955, suburbanization was rapidly under way. With downtown school enrollment dipping to just 251, the Temple was faced with a dilemma: should it cater to the suburbanites, who needed a nearby religious school, or to older downtown residents who still attended services? The leadership compromised: it voted to build a school branch in the suburb of Newton, on the condition that worship would continue downtown. In effect, Mishkan Tefila now had two congregations: aging downtowners raised on worship as religion's fulcrum, and suburbanites focused on educating children. Whereas the Roxbury synagogue had begun as a sanctuary (1925) and only later (1929) added a school, the Newton branch began as a school (in 1956) and only afterward (1958) added a sanctuary.

In suburban religion, then, worship virtually ceased to matter. But congregants (mostly from eastern Europe, lacking experience of glorious worship anyway) expected synagogues to 'raise their children Jewish.' By the mid 1960s and 1970s, with younger baby-boomers going through school and older boomers already in College, a second

37 Ibid., p. 21.
38 In general, worship attendance is overstated by as much as 50 percent. See Lawrence A. Hoffman, 'From Common Cold to Uncommon Healing,' *CCAR Journal*, Spring 1994, p. 27, n. 13.

religious imperative opened up: social justice. Here was a topic born of marches in Alabama, Vietnam despair, and riots in the cities—all of which found ready resonance among Jews whose parents had marched as socialists, and whose children were potential military draftees. The synagogues of suburbia redefined Jewish religion as learning and social action. Worship hardly happened.

In many ways, Percival Goodman is the architect who best represented the new age. Though he was ultimately to design some fifty-four synagogues in twenty states, the design that established him as the premier architect of the post-war era is Congregation Beth El in Providence (*page 178*), which took shape over the course of six torturous years, from 1947 to 1952. Beth El remains centered around its magnificent sanctuary. The same can be said of the new Mishkan Tefila, which Goodman turned to in 1955. But whereas the Roxbury sanctuary had held 1600, Goodman's Newton sanctuary held only 800, and Beth El too had room for only 900. But both sanctuaries boasted expandable walls, allowing Mishkan Tefila to accommodate 2000 and Beth El 1600 on the High Holy Days.

If the displacement of the sanctuary by the school wing and social hall was the first innovation in suburbia, the second was the movable walls. The expandable sanctuary design—originally a 1945 Cecil Moore experiment in Tucson—was popularized by Eric Mendelson,[39] and used ubiquitously by Goodman. As it turned out, even the smaller worship spaces proved far too large. But they had been designed not necessarily to be filled. Even Jews who did not attend worship wanted to be proud of the worship space that they did not attend. Think of coffee-table books that provide the semblance of culture just by being there. You may even thumb through them on occasion. So too, post-World War II synagogues had coffee-table sanctuaries, that could be entered on occasion, and if not thumbed through, walked through, admiringly.

So even though Goodman recognized the changing function of synagogue space as a whole, he paid careful attention to the sanctuaries, at which he was a genius. He had familiarized himself with the Liturgical Movement in Catholicism, an attempt, even before Vatican II, to replace such medievalisms as private masses and a passive congregation with full congregational presence and participation. To the Catholic situation, Goodman juxtaposed the I-Thou theology of Martin Buber, maintaining that the very essence of Jewish prayer was the congregational presence to God and to each other.[40] That led him to see the ark as the focal point for Jewish prayer. It was, he thought, a recapitulation of Sinai (a claim, incidentally, that would later be demonstrated by a close textual reading of the liturgy itself).[41] By experimenting with a semi-circular seating plan, he brought the congregation into more intimate space with the bimah, and (as Buber would have it) face to face with each other (innovations that anticipated the search for spirituality in the 1990s).[42] But he kept in mind also the new priorities of education and suburban socializing. He thereby became an architect of choice for synagogues intent on a brilliantly designed worship space even if it went largely unfilled except on special occasions.

39 See Sussman, 'Suburbanization,' p. 40–41.

40 Percival and Paul Goodman, 'Modern Artist as Synagogue Builder,' p. 53.

41 Ruth Langer, 'From Study of Scripture to Reenactment of Sinai,': The Emergence of the Synagogue Torah Service,' *Worship* 72, 1998, pp. 43–67.

42 Evelyn L. Greenberg, 'Percival Goodman's Synagogues,' *Jewish Art* 19/20, 1993–1994, p. 47.

The problem of an unfilled sanctuary was solved, in part, in the 1960s, when synagogues became bar/bat mitzvah mills. Already in Germany, Jews had begun replacing bar mitzvah with confirmation, a group ritual that corresponded to normative church practice in the surrounding Lutheran world.[43] Here too, it was commonplace for German Reform Jewish men in the 1950s and '60s to report that they had never celebrated a bar mitzvah. But eastern European Jews who reached adulthood in the post-war years and then joined Reform synagogues wanted a bar mitzvah for their children. The rabbis acceded, and not just because they missed the bar mitzvah rite. Reinstating it solved several problems at once. It appealed to the eastern-European nostalgia for tradition; as bat mitzvah, it could be extended to girls as well; as a precondition for bar/bat mitzvah, it could motivate children to attend religious school; and guests invited to attend the ritual would fill empty sanctuaries. A parallel development occurred in Conservative synagogues, which had never banished bar mitzvah, but which found it, nonetheless, playing the additional role of bringing people to services that would otherwise have been largely unattended.

All across America, then, a different kind of synagogue marked suburbia. It featured different zones of activity.[44] Separate from the rest of the synagogue, the school wing was provided with a private entrance where parents could drop off children without coming into contact with the sanctuary space. Other self-enclosed zones included an office area for an increasingly complex synagogue staff, clergy, and professional corps; a youth lounge set off where teenagers wouldn't have to encounter adults; a library (usually empty), tucked away someplace in the internal bowels of the synagogue; a social hall (behind removable walls and abutting the sanctuary, so as to serve an overflow crowd on High Holy days); and meeting rooms for the board and committees. The sanctuary was still aesthetically central, but of diminished functional importance. Worship played a minor role relative to childhood education, committee meetings, and social programing.

We should differentiate Reform from Conservative Judaism here. Reform synagogues still featured Friday night services, an innovation, as we saw, that was designed to prevent a conflict with business hours. The small group of regulars who attended might indeed have reported an experience of spirituality. But most people came for other reasons altogether: celebrating fifth-grade Shabbat, perhaps, or to listen to an interesting speaker. Programing, that is, replaced worship as the standard Shabbat evening activity. On Saturday mornings no one came at all, unless they were guests of the bar/bat mitzvah family, or board members shanghaied to present the requisite congregational gift to the boy or girl being celebrated.

The Conservative Movement had been founded as the acculturation vehicle for eastern European Jews, paralleling the Reform Movement's role for Jews from central Europe. This took the form of a traditional service with a modern aesthetic (as pioneering sociologist Marshall Sklare put it) mediating 'the feeling of both alienation and nostalgia,' toward the past, and instituting the norms of modern

43 Stephanie E. Alexander, *Standing at the Altar: Reimagining the Significance of Bar/Bat Mitzvah*, Unpublished Rabbinic dissertation, Hebrew Union College – Jewish Institute of Religion, New York, 2003, p. 39.

44 See Lawrence A. Hoffman, 'Zoning Out and Tuning In to Education for Jewish Journeys,' *Jewish Education News* 23:1, Winter, 2002, pp. 24–26.

middle-class worship.[45] But already in the 1920s, some Conservative rabbis were giving up on making synagogue life dependent on worship above all. The most noteworthy response was a new kind of institution: the synagogue as community center, a place not only for prayer, but for any activity that might bring Jews together. Its origins actually went back to Reform rabbis of the 1880s, who wanted to recognize the important component of Jews just getting together—partly because central European immigration was coming to an end, and its German-Jewish culture was becoming a thing of the past.[46] The idea was reintroduced more or less officially under the influence of theologian Mordecai Kaplan, who had been teaching at the Jewish Theological Seminary since 1909. But evaluations were not all positive, since assembling Jews to swim or play bridge did not translate into personal religious commitment. In any event, the depression cut off funds required to expand the synagogue-center system.[47]

Suburban Conservative rabbis faced their own problem with the diminishing role of worship. Usually, their congregations had already instituted Friday night services, as in Reform.[48] Unlike Reform however—and contrary to the experience at Mishkan Tefila, apparently—Friday night became increasingly peripheral to Saturday morning, which bore the brunt of attracting the regulars. But Conservative synagogues too were eventually swamped with visitors for the bar/bat mitzvah. The service even changed to fit the congregational 'audience.' Shabbat morning worship has three parts: a lengthy Morning (*shacharit*) Service; then the reading of Torah; and finally, a short Additional (*musaf*) Service. When guests began deliberately arriving late, just in time for the Torah reading which featured the bar/bat mitzvah child, it became commonplace for the cantor to run swiftly and perfunctorily through the prior Morning Service, and then later, with a captive audience present, to elongate the Additional Service with extensive cantorial and choir music. Again, some people found the high artistry of the service spiritual. But most did not, and except for the High Holy Days and bar/bat mitzvah events, they stopped attending synagogue altogether. (Still an issue, the current response—itself controversial—has been the establishment of alternative services outside the main sanctuary where regulars can congregate to pray as they wish.)

What we have called in this book the heroic style of architecture was just a magnification of what has already been described. Here too, suburbanization was eating away at membership attendance; here too b'nai mitzvah and their guests hijacked the otherwise empty sanctuary. Heroic sanctuaries were built on a vast and awesome level anyway—modern versions of the cathedrals from the prior era. As spaces they take your breath away. As places for worship in an era demanding intimacy, they mostly fail—though who knows? Their time may come again. The baby-boomers are aging, and it is not yet certain what the next generation will want.

In any case, some of the heroic visionaries anticipated the search for spirituality that was to set in by the century's end. The best example may be Frank Lloyd Wright's Beth Sholom Synagogue in Elkins Park, Pennsylvania (*page 174*).

45   Marshall Sklare, *Conservative Judaism*, Free Press, Glencoe, 1955, p. 75.

46   Cf. David Kaufman, *Shul With a Pool*, Hanover NH, 1999, pp. 20–34.

47   See Jack Wertheimer, 'The Conservative Synagogue,' in idem., ed., *The American Synagogue: A Sanctuary Transformed*, Cambridge University Press, Cambridge, 1987, p. 121.

48   Sklare, *Conservative Judaism*, gives the figures: 84 percent of small congregations (100 families or less); 36 percent of large congregations (over 500 families).

Beth Sholom was a prominent Conservative congregation in Philadelphia. With religious school attendance down from a high of 600 to 125, and the fear that younger families who had already left the center city would start a rival synagogue, it established a suburban branch in 1949. Like Newton's Mishkan Tefila, the branch catered to education and social events, with a large school wing and even a pool in the basement. Here too, worship was the last thing the Temple worried about. For six years, services were held for dwindling numbers of attendees in the downtown sanctuary, or, sometimes, in the branch social hall—hardly built with spirituality in mind.

By 1954, however, missing a sanctuary for what was going to become the main synagogue site, Rabbi Mortimer Cohen (1894–1972) turned to Wright, a perfect choice, in that he appreciated Cohen's dual commitment to Jewish particularism and to universalism. Cohen's perspective is evident in his invitation to Wright to design 'a symbol for generations to come of the American and Jewish Spirit, a House of Prayer in which all may come to know themselves better as children of the living God.'[49] He had probably assimilated this view from Mordecai Kaplan, who, as we saw, was the guiding voice behind the synagogue-center movement. Kaplan conceived of Judaism as a civilization, arguing that Jews here shared an amalgam of two cultures: Judaism and America. While celebrating the uniqueness of Jewish identity, he rejected the concept of a chosen people, and located Judaism within the larger tale of human evolution.

Wright seemed to understand the particularistic side of the Jewish narrative. Typifying the modernist disavowal of classical symbols, he sought instead some natural and central symbol inherent in his subject—in this case, the synagogue. 'At last, a great symbol,' he declared. 'Rabbi Mortimer J. Cohen gave me the idea of a 'traveling Mt. Sinai'—a mountain of light.'[50] Goodman had found that symbolism in the ark. Wright chose the entire synagogue building.

But like his rabbinic mentor Cohen, he saw even Sinai in universal terms. At the groundbreaking, Wright announced, 'Call it Jewish, call it Methodist, call it any name you please, what's the difference, and those differences are going to grow smaller, more insignificant as the great significance of faith in beauty pays off.'[51] Both Wright and Cohen were striving for the same thing, but for different reasons. Wright, nearing the end of his career and having been passed over several times for synagogue commissions, wanted at last to make his mark on a synagogue. Cohen wanted to demonstrate that he and his congregation had 'arrived' in suburbia as both Jews and Americans.

Wright's design was fully suburban in its inclusion of gathering spaces in the form of lounges inside the building's entrance. Here was a synagogue where talking was not only permitted, but encouraged. For the average Shabbat, Wright included a small chapel for 250 worshipers; and then there was the main sanctuary. When Cohen had rhapsodized about his synagogue becoming 'A new thing—the American spirit wedded to the spirit of Israel,' he did not have 1990s-style spirituality in mind. But Wright was prescient in his recognition of the coldness that theater-style seating

49 Cited in G.M.N. Goodwin, 'Wright's Beth Sholom Synagogue,' *American Jewish History* 86:3, 1998, p. 338.

50 *Architectural Forum*, June 1959; cited Mortimer J. Cohen, *Beth Sholom Synagogue* [issued by the synagogue itself in 1959], p. 2.

51 Goodwin, 'Beth Sholom,' p. 341.

entails. Though large (1030 seats), his sanctuary anticipated the search for intimacy, even in grandeur, that would become the hallmark of baby-boomer spirituality. His conception of Israel gathering around Sinai led to an interior design whereby rows of chairs sit angularly to each other rather than in theater-style pews facing a stage-like box of a bimah. When he was done, Wright had manufactured a brilliantly designed sanctuary, large but intimate, with a thrust- bimah, and crosscutting rows of seats offsetting social distance between bimah and worshipers, and among worshipers themselves.

It is worth noting the decisive role that at least some rabbis played in those post-war years, and the extent to which even they had little interest in worship and spirituality. All three rabbis—Braude in Providence, Kazis in Boston, and Cohen in Philadelphia—were noted for their erudition and scholarship. Judaism, for them, was an academic thing; study was central; education imperative; and worship tangential. But these were modern scholars, who appreciated the arts no less than midrash or the Bible itself, the written texts whence religious artists derived their ideas. Synagogue design was an artistic idea, to be appreciated no less than the word-play of a midrashic passage or the subtlety of a talmudic commentary. Shape had little to do with worship, which the three rabbis neither understood nor valued overly much. Yet at least in Providence and Elkins Park, they almost singlehandedly chose the architect. And all three used their scholarship to influence their synagogues' architectural design. For Rabbis Braude and Kazis, the answer arrived with the emerging Percival Goodman; for Cohen, it was the iconoclastic and mature Frank Lloyd Wright.

SPIRITUALITY AT THE TURN OF THE MILLENNIUM

Our story comes to an end with the maturation of the very baby-boomers for whom suburban synagogues were built; and the greying of their parents who built them. They represent a fourth American generation.[52]

The first two generations were the founders of American Judaism, both Sephardim and Ashkenazim, who arrived intent on demonstrating that Jews could be good Americans. Since citizenship presupposed Judaism as religion, and since American Protestant culture made worship central to religion, they designed sanctuary-centered synagogues in which some form of spirituality, we may assume, was sought and attained. By contrast, the third generation, suburbanites, represented eastern European Jews for whom worship was marginal. As Americans responding to Eisenhower's Cold War plea to join a church or synagogue; as Jews still needing confirmation that they had arrived (this time, in the Protestant suburbs); and as parents of the largest cohort of children in American history; they sought synagogues with coffee-table sanctuaries—beauty on display, but rarely visited in depth.

52 For the generational theme, see Lawrence A. Hoffman, *The Journey Home*, Beacon Press, Boston, 2002, pp. 189–214.

All three generations corresponded to parallel trends in American religion generally. The very first immigrants arrived in a century so religious that wars of religion still plagued Europe and came close to dominating America too; and they grew up in the colonial era that had featured the first American religious awakening, with famed New England preachers like Jonathan Edwards and George Whitefield. Their synagogues mirrored churches where preaching, praying and devotional reading predominated.[53] The central European migration too coincided with a religious awakening, the second one, that began in Kentucky in 1801, reached a zenith in 1830, but continued for decades thereafter.

There are signs that religious worship lost something of its radiance by the 1890s, years that were known for their social gospel more than their evangelical fervor. Well into the twentieth century, fortunes from the age of the robber barons went into grandiose structures of all kinds, religion included, and people still went to church (and synagogue), at least for musical edification and moral instruction. Mishkan Tefila's Roxbury home typified such structures then. The depression and the war took up all of America's energy from 1929 to 1945, but the post-war years brought suburban religion to Christians no less than Jews. Already in 1949, although the population rose only by 1.5 percent, the increase in religious bodies was double that (3 percent).[54] Methodist or Presbyterian neighborhood churches look much the same as Reform or Conservative synagogues: large school wings, meeting halls, and relatively small sanctuaries unequipped with the pipe organs and marble that only the gilded age could afford. Our story now arrives at generation four, again a mirror of American religion as a whole: the baby-boomers, and their quest, as mature adults, for spirituality.

The boomers' accent on self-determination and self-expression should be seen as part of a larger critique of American institutionalism and conformism in general. Raised to distrust the military-industrial complex, and scornful of their parents' suburban values, they remain critical of whatever smacks of the staid and sheltered age of Ozzie and Harriet. As 1970s youth groupers, they experimented with liturgy, denounced their movement prayer books and invented mimeographed 'creative liturgy.'[55] Now, at fifty or so, they accuse organized religion of maintaining synagogues with prayer services but without spirituality.

In Christian liturgy, the dichotomy is often framed as a distinction between 'cathedral' and 'monastic' prayer.[56] Cathedral prayer is the standard publicly prayed offices of the church (Jews would call them the mandatory daily services), led by ordained officials, consisting of praise or petition, and dependent on the details of 'proper' praying procedure. Monastic prayer is the opposite: personal devotion appropriate at any and all times; and pursued without ordained leaders. It is directed inward, not just as a service to God, but for the spiritual wellbeing of the worshiper; and is unencumbered by regulations. The two can occur together, as when standard daily services are pursued with inward intent. And they may be so completely intertwined that they are hard to separate. Historically, however, for many reasons—

53 From Sidney E. Ahlstrom, *A Religious History of the American People*, Yale University Press, New Haven, 1972, p. 287.
54 Ellwood, *1950: Crossroads of American Life*, p. 99.
55 See Lawrence A. Hoffman, 'Creative Liturgy,' *Jewish Spectator* 40:4, Winter 1975, 42–49.
56 Cf. Paul F. Bradshaw, *Two Ways of Praying*, Abingdon Press, Nashville, 1995; idem., 'Cathedral and Monsatic: What's in a Name?' *Worship* 77:4, 2003, pp. 341–353.

the invention of printing, the growth of individualism, and the romantic movement—the two were separated, with cathedral prayer becoming what happens in most churches, and monastic prayer what people take up on their own in search of the spiritual.

Though the nomenclature may differ, Jewish prayer has much the same history. Judaism has no monastic orders, but it does have parallels in German mystics, kabbalistic masters, and Hasidim of the twelfth, sixteenth, and eighteenth centuries respectively. All of these, however, would have claimed the possibility of the spiritual in synagogue prayer as well as independent meditation. When, then, did spirituality separate from synagogue prayer?

The argument here is that except for the suburban period, to which we are now reacting, it never did. Every form of synagogue worship has posited some form of spirituality (with or without the name) that its devotees sought and frequently found. Only in the post-war era did spirituality lose its communal institutional way, and only because worship did also. What worship there was got folded into a larger suburban agenda: prayer as an aid to education and social justice. The revival of prayer as something spiritual today should occasion no surprise. Part of the baby-boomer critique was precisely the charge that their parents' suburban synagogues knew no spirituality. Not realizing that spirituality's absence was the anomaly, not the norm, these critics hardly thought to look deeper into Judaism. Rather, they investigated spiritual practices of the east. But America in general, and Judaism in particular, are now in the throes of a third religious awakening, the focus of which is the revival of worship with spirituality at its core.

Like other forms of spirituality, however, this one too is conditioned by the culture that spawns it. It is distinctively baby-boom oriented: the search for meaning, by a generation that saw established orders of meaning disappear overnight; and for community, by people who have lost extended families, neighborhoods and marriages, but who revel in the very idea of community coming together. Singing together is in; so is intimacy rather than distance; active, not passive worship; understated simplicity, not overstated elegance; and the wonder of nature, not industrially produced design. Architects are called to conceptualize spaces where these considerations are primary.

Two trends are evident: the development of small chapels outside the main sanctuary (which is virtually abandoned, except for 'state' occasions like bar/bat mitzvah services and High Holy Day worship); and new or renovated sanctuaries that reflect intimacy, natural light, simple design, and no social distance between clergy and participants (so that both may actively pray together). Our book aptly illustrates these new developments: intimate chapels, accesses through walks in nature, lowered bimahs, circular seating, and so on. Liturgically, worship practices are moving simultaneously toward training clergy in a fitting style of prayer, and providing prayer books designed to make that prayer more likely.

I have devoted more attention to American Reform and Conservative Judaism than I have Orthodoxy, since until relatively recently, American history has favored their demographic success. Their very numbers gave them the commercial means to participate in the quintessential American religious project: a building for neighborhood worship. The founder of Reconstructionism, Mordecai Kaplan, has also figured significantly in this narrative, both ideologically (his influence on Rabbi Mortimer Cohen) and institutionally (in the concept of a synagogue center). And Sephardi Orthodox founders have been duly noted too. But Ashkenazi Orthodox Jews have their own story to tell, two developments of which are especially pertinent to my focus on architecture and spirituality today.

First, there is the obvious Orthodox success story, rooted in a trend toward 'public Orthodoxy.' Until the 1990s, many people who claimed to be Orthodox, acted in no way publicly to demonstrate that commitment. Many were not personally Orthodox at all—they just belonged to Orthodox congregations, preferring (when they did attend services) to pray in the Orthodox mode. By the 1990s, however, that was changing. Demographically, Orthodoxy slipped from 11 percent of the American public in 1970 to 6 percent in 1990,[57] not because Orthodoxy was getting weaker, but because it was getting stronger, forcing anyone who was not serious about an Orthodox way of life to take up ideological residence elsewhere—usually with Conservative Judaism. Orthodoxy too, however, was caught up in the quest for intimacy—helped along by the naturally democratic nature of Orthodox prayer (anyone can lead it). Moreover, serious Orthodox commitment requires living near the synagogue and walking there on Shabbat, so Orthodox Judaism has retained neighborhoods and even the sense of extended families—natural communities that other Jews (along with Americans at large) have lost. So in places like Riverdale, New York, and the Lubavitch congregation featured in these pages (*page 252*), we have seen vibrant Orthodox synagogues celebrating community, intimacy and the other characteristics of baby-boom oriented spirituality.

But even small and intimate Orthodox synagogues do not always bring the requisite spirituality. Many Orthodox Jews do not customarily use the word 'spirituality.' They speak instead of the *davening* (praying) being good or bad. Good *davening* is, presumably, spiritual *davening*. Yet anecdotal evidence suggests that even the good *davening* is often seen as lacking spirituality, and in many places, *davening* is perfunctory, but accompanied by extended discussion of the Torah reading, which makes study (not prayer) the service's spiritual center. Architecture alone will not solve this problem. At stake is the extent to which Orthodox interpretation of Jewish law will allow innovation. Music is critical here, as elsewhere, and for better or for worse, one cutting edge of the Orthodox frontier at the moment is a debate on whether the so-called Carlebach music (an upbeat participational style named after its founder, the late Shlomo Carlebach) may replace or even supplement traditional Jewish musical modes.

57 Jeffrey Gurock, *Fluidity to Rigidity*, p. 37, n. 114. At this writing the more recent survey from the turn of the century is still being hotly debated. The Orthodox presence is clearly higher than it was in 1990, but the exact number is uncertain.

Some Jews, however, have resisted all the trends adduced here. The modern search for spirituality, as for artistic or empowering architectural space, is unimportant to them. The following concluding story comes to mind as an important corrective to everything I have been saying.

Several years ago, I visited one of the last remaining Jewish bookstores on New York's Lower East side. With me was Professor Michael Signer, a colleague and friend who teaches Jewish Studies at the University of Notre Dame. While Michael collected one book after another for purchase, I settled on a single volume, which I bought and began to read.

As Michael finally finished, I noticed that for the first time in the entire afternoon, other customers were entering the store. One settled into a chair to inspect a book; another browsed through an entire shelf; yet a third stood motionless before a blank wall. As the February sun set and the store owner rang up the sale, it dawned on me: the new arrivals were not customers. They were Orthodox Jews gathered for late afternoon and evening prayer. The bookstore was their regular 'sanctuary.'

As this thought sprang to my mind, the man facing the wall began leading the prayers *sotto voce*—in that distinctive 'muttering' style that constitutes traditionalistic Jewish worship. The man in the chair went about his recitation while still thumbing through his book. The man at the bookshelf continued browsing. Most astonishing of all, the store owner managed to pray and ring up the sales simultaneously.

'*Ashrei yoshvei veisekha* [Happy are they who dwell in Your house]—$29.95; *od y'hall'lukha selah* [They praise You continually]—$18.95...'

Then another voice joined in. The man who was both praying and reading his book managed (without missing a word of prayer) to ask the owner who Michael and I were. He used Yiddish, expecting we would not understand.

'Who are these Jews? They seem to read holy books but they don't seem very Jewish.'

'*Ashrei yoshvei veisekha* [Happy are they who dwell in Your house]—$29.95,' came the reply. 'They are visitors; one of them teaches at some Reform seminary; *od y'hall'lukha selah* [They praise You continually]—$18.95. The other comes from a Catholic university somewhere...'

Later, Michael and I left without having exchanged a word with any of the other worshipers. To the best of my knowledge, none of them said anything to each other either. But they had taken the time to do their religious duty.

Had I been an anthropologist taking field notes, I would have observed that mixing prayer with secular conversation and computations of book sales would be anathema to most of the Jewish groups discussed above. The worshipers in this tiny storefront had probably never even heard of sacred space. But like many Orthodox

Jews who take time after every meal to hurry through several pages of the *Birkat Hamazon* ('Grace After Meals'), even while deftly continuing table conversations with those who have little idea what they are even doing, they are engaged in 'part of a larger packet of rituals, whose meaning is derived from its being perceived as the imposition of order and the demand for obedience by God.'[58]

Am I prepared to say that the storefront worship was not, in its own way, spiritual? Not at all. Spirituality is hardly an objective quality of prayer. It varies with the system of which prayer is a part. If we now name it 'spiritual,' it is only by the imposition of a term that is alien to historical Jewish consciousness, but which, in our time, may be meaningfully applied nonetheless, as an indication that Jewish prayer fulfills the criteria of what prayer is said to be all about in contemporary America. But ultimately, spirituality is in the eye of the beholder.

58 Charles S. Liebman, *Deceptive Images: Toward a Redefinition of American Judaism*, Transaction Books, New Brunswick, 1988, p. 48.

SYNAGOGUE ARCHITECTURE IN AMERICA

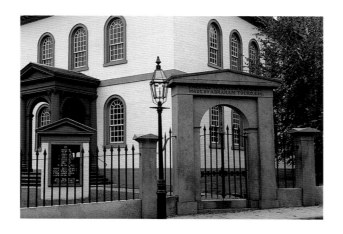

TOURO SYNAGOGUE | NEWPORT, RI

PETER HARRISON

BUILT 1763

The oldest existing synagogue in America, Touro Synagogue is one of the most celebrated examples of eighteenth-century Georgian architecture in America. It demonstrates how early American Jewish congregations avidly embraced local architectural styles for their synagogues.

A group of Sephardic Jews who originally came from Holland and the Dutch colonies settled in North America in the mid-seventeenth century. In 1658, thirteen Sephardic Jews arrived in the burgeoning port town of Newport, Rhode Island. Most believe that the Touro Jews came directly from Curaçao in the West Indies, though they may have come with the group from Holland, or from New York, where a Jewish congregation, Shearith Israel, had recently been established.

Founded by Roger Williams on the tenets of religious tolerance, the Rhode Island colony was a logical place for Jewish immigrants. After they settled, the original Jewish community grew as more Jews came to America, including a group of Ashkenazi Jews who arrived in the 1750s. At that time, the congregation undertook the task of building the second synagogue ever to be constructed in America. The congregation's funds were supplemented by support from Sephardic congregations in New York, Jamaica, Curaçao, Surinam and London.

Architect Peter Harrison, renowned for building many notable colonial structures throughout the Northeast, designed a synagogue that fit into the local landscape. Like most architecture of the period, Touro's design and details were largely inspired by English pattern books. The synagogue is a simple, two-story brick structure that is elevated on a sandstone base. While historians consider John Webb's Whitehall Palace

OPPOSITE: *The sanctuary.*
ABOVE: *Entry faces east and is placed at an oblique angle to the street.*

in London to be the most significant influence on Harrison's design, the modest façade recalls the congregational meetinghouses that were common in America at the time.

From the outside, the Touro Synagogue can barely be recognized as a Jewish house of worship. There are no exterior details or clues, aside from the fact that the building is placed on an acute angle so that it may face east, toward Jerusalem, in accordance with Jewish tradition. The inside of the sanctuary, on the other hand, incorporates elements from two venerated Sephardic synagogues, the Sephardic Synagogue in Amsterdam (1675), and the Sephardic Bevis Marks Synagogue in London (1701). Like them, Touro has 12 imposing columns that represent the 12 tribes of Israel. These columns support the upstairs gallery. The reading platform is placed at the center of the worship space and the seating lines the north and south walls facing the ark and bimah, as was common for traditional Sephardic synagogues.

LEFT: *Central bimah with an ark designed like a finely carved cabinet with the Ten Commandments above.*
ABOVE: *Entry façade.*

KAHAL KADOSH BETH ELOHIM SYNAGOGUE
CHARLESTON, SC

CYRUS L. WARNER

BUILT 1840

Congregation Kahal Kadosh Beth Elohim is the second-oldest congregation in the United States, and its Greek Revival synagogue building is the oldest American synagogue in continuous use. The congregation's founders arrived in Charleston as early as 1695, lured by the city's abundant commercial opportunities—and its relatively liberal religious policies. Unlike some other American colonies, Carolina allowed Jews to congregate and pray freely.

The architecture and organization of the congregation's successive homes reflect the evolution of Charleston's Jewish community, as well as general changes in American Jewry over the years. A century after they arrived in Charleston, the congregants had become well-assimilated Charleston residents, and their first house of worship was designed accordingly. Built in 1794, the original building was a small, ecclesiastical-looking structure with a steeple and pitched roof. The synagogue's church-like exterior fit in well with the architectural context of Charleston, whereas the building's interior proclaimed the Jews' singular religion and culture. Inside the sanctuary, the seating was arranged around a central ark and bimah according to Sephardic tradition.

Beth Elohim is considered to be the birthplace of the Reform Movement in America, an indigenous movement whose innovations paralleled the liturgical changes that were taking place in Germany at the turn of the nineteenth century. In 1824, some of the membership began to demand changes to Americanize the services and make them more like those of the Christian church. Their demands included a greater sense of formality, replacing the use of Ladino (a mix of Hebrew and Spanish) with

OPPOSITE: *View of front façade from the entrance gates.*
ABOVE: *View of entry from the street.*

TOP: *View of sanctuary from the balcony.*

MIDDLE: *View of the rounded mahogany ark from the central aisle. The ark was relocated from the congregation's first synagogue, which was destroyed by fire (page 37).*

BOTTOM: *View from the bimah.*

ABOVE: *Choir loft with an organ that affirms the congregation's acceptance of Protestant liturgical traditions.*

English, and the elimination of 'repetitious and superfluous' matter in the services. When the larger congregation refused to make these modifications, this group created their own Reformed Society of Israelites, adopted dramatic liturgical changes, and began to worship separately. After nine years, however, this progressive organization disbanded, and its members returned to the Beth Elohim congregation. The community's acceptance of liturgical reform fluctuated for decades, but eventually the reformers would win out. By 1893, the congregation officially accepted the Reform prayer book.

The current Beth Elohim building replaced the first synagogue, which was destroyed by fire in 1838. In 1880, 40 years after the second synagogue was built, the community replaced the traditional Sephardic seating with family pews. This new organization enabled men and women to sit together as they did in Christian churches, and gave the congregants a feeling of American respectability. The bimah, which had been in the center of the sanctuary, was moved to its present position next to the ark.

LLOYD STREET SYNAGOGUE
(BALTIMORE HEBREW CONGREGATION)
BALTIMORE, MD

ROBERT CAREY LONG, JR.

BUILT 1845

Like many other American civic and religious buildings of the period, the Lloyd Street Synagogue was built in the Greek Revival style. With its four fluted columns supporting a portico, the synagogue looked like a Doric temple when it appeared in the heart of the city's Jewish neighborhood. Architect Robert Carey Long had recently designed two Greek Revival churches in Baltimore. The rounded windows on the façade of the Lloyd Street Synagogue, however, offered a slight deviation from the classical model. More significantly, the Jewish stars that were set within the windows marked the first known use (in an American synagogue) of the Star of David—the ubiquitous icon now recognized universally as the symbol of the Jews.

The Lloyd Street Synagogue was built in 1845 by the Baltimore Hebrew Congregation, a group of German Jews who had immigrated to Maryland in the first half of the nineteenth century. In its early days, the Maryland colony had a relatively small Jewish population, given that colonists were required to declare Christ as their savior in order to settle there. Upon the establishment of the state of Maryland, Jews were constitutionally prohibited from entering or holding public office, until the so-called 'Jew Bill' was passed in 1826, permanently lifting the ban and bringing Maryland's Jews into public life.

Inside, the building's sanctuary is simple and unadorned, aside from the beautiful bimah, which is located in the center of the room. The hand-carved ark is by far the most lavish element, although the current ark is actually a smaller replica of the original. The pews have doors that shut and lock, a feature that also appears in

OPPOSITE: *Entry colonnade had originally included Hebrew inscriptions, since painted over.*
ABOVE: *View of entry prior to restoration.*

some churches of the time. It is thought that locking pews—beyond supplying a measure of privacy and 'ownership' of particular pews—may have been used to keep out drafts, thus keeping congregants warm in the winter months.

OPPOSITE: *Sanctuary with a traditional women's gallery and non-traditional locked pews for men below.*
ABOVE: *Ark and bimah.*

The Jewish Museum of Maryland was founded in 1960 to rescue and restore the synagogue, which had been abandoned by the congregation in the late 1880s (the building was then converted for use as a Catholic church; after the turn of the century an Orthodox congregation moved in). Today the Museum offers exhibits and Jewish programs in an adjacent building, along with tours of the synagogue.

ISAAC M. WISE TEMPLE (PLUM STREET TEMPLE)
CINCINNATI, OH

JAMES KEY WILSON

BUILT 1866

Built in 1866, the Isaac M. Wise Temple, with its minarets and lacy ornamentation, ushered in the so-called Moorish style for synagogues in the United States; soon thereafter, the style—championed by both Jews and non-Jews as the most 'Jewish' style of architecture—became ubiquitous for American synagogues. Not until the turn of the century did its popularity begin to wane.

In America, the Moorish style had first been used in 1848 when Leopold Eidlitz designed a Saracenic-influenced villa in Connecticut for showman P.T. Barnum; Barnum dubiously named his new estate 'Iranistan.' First in Europe, and then in the United States, exoticized architectural motifs—influenced by the experience of European colonialism—were imported to bring a sense of wonder and beauty to residential, civic, and institutional buildings alike.

Given that exotic architectural styles had become popular in American secular architecture, the use of the Moorish style in a synagogue suggested both that Jews were a group apart—a separate ethnicity with Middle Eastern roots, an 'Other' in Western society—and that they were fashionable, assimilated Americans.

At the Isaac M. Wise Temple, the most obviously Islamic features of the façade are its two minarets, one rising from each side. The long, slender forms with pointed windows are typically used in mosques to provide a lofty place from which the Muslim call to prayer can be made. The alternating use of brick and masonry on the façade is another common Islamic motif. However, the interior of the synagogue is the place where the Moorish style is most boldly implemented. Vibrant patterns cover every surface and niche of the sanctuary. The ark at the far end of the space is also replete with ornament, and its physical shape mimics the façade of the synagogue, with a miniature minaret capping each side.

OPPOSITE: *Sanctuary adorned with vibrant Islamic ornament.*
ABOVE: *Plum Street façade.*

Ironically, the building's architect, James Key Wilson, was known as 'the architect of the Gothic revival in Cincinnati,' and there are certainly Gothic aspects to this synagogue. Gothic elements include the three pointed archways and rose windows of the façade, and the T-shape basilica plan, which had been commonly used in Gothic churches.

When construction was finished, Rabbi Isaac M. Wise, the rabbi of the congregation and the central organizing force behind the early American reform movement, called the synagogue an 'Alhambra Temple,' referring to the Alhambra, the Islamic palace built in Granada, Spain in the fourteenth century. The congregation's new temple, Wise suggested by the comparison, exemplified the perfect synagogue architecture.

CENTRAL SYNAGOGUE | NEW YORK, NY

HENRY FERNBACH

BUILT 1872

New York City's Central Synagogue contributes significantly to the legacy of Moorish Revival architecture. Built in 1872, soon after the Plum Street Temple in Cincinnati (*page 108*), its design similarly illustrates the way that Eastern imagery was often applied to synagogue buildings without changing their typical massing or formal arrangement. Like Plum Street, Central Synagogue's decoration is predominantly Moorish, while its plan is a typical Gothic basilica.

The Moorish style was first used for synagogues in Europe, and the Dohany Street Synagogue in Budapest (1854–8), the largest Jewish house of worship in Europe, was one of the first buildings to legitimize the Moorish style for synagogue architecture. Dohany Street Synagogue subsequently inspired synagogues that were built in Hungary and across Europe. By the 1890s the great majority of synagogues, both in the United States and abroad, featured Islamic motifs. All types of congregations, ranging from Reform to Orthodox, employed the 'Oriental' lexicon, and Central Synagogue is one of the most celebrated examples of the Moorish style in the United States.

The architect of Central Synagogue, Henry Fernbach, kept current with European architectural movements, and borrowed heavily from Dohany's façade for his design. Many of the building's significant features, including its towering minarets and lavish Arabic ceiling mosaics, were adopted from Dohany. Central's sanctuary is a rich combination of stars, lines, circles, and fleurettes, rendered in 69 different shades of red, tan, gold, brown, blue, and apricot. These patterns were created by more than 5000 separate stencils, and they were applied to the walls by hand. Despite the abundance of decoration (hardly a surface has been left bare), the room is not overly lush, since so much of the ornamentation is stenciled rather than carved.

OPPOSITE: Horseshoe arch in upper gallery.
ABOVE: One of two bulbous domes, crowned by a golden five-pointed star.
FOLLOWING PAGES: Ornate façade of the synagogue contrasts with New York City's sleek office buildings along Lexington Avenue.

Although the congregation is Reform, the architect included a balcony with additional seating. While Orthodox congregations have traditionally used balconies in synagogues in order to separate women from men, the Central Synagogue congregation had mixed seating, using the balcony merely for additional seating on High Holidays, when attendance customarily swelled. The balcony's presence at Central Synagogue is an echo of tradition in view of the liturgical reforms that were then rapidly taking place in parts of the Jewish community.

A city, state, and national landmark, Central Synagogue was severely damaged by fire in August 1998, and it has since been fully restored by Hardy Holzman Pfeiffer Associates. As part of the restoration, flexible seating and a movable reading table were inserted at the front of the sanctuary. This reorganization creates a traditional seating arrangement that makes smaller services in the sanctuary feel more inclusive and intimate.

OPPOSITE: *Sanctuary as viewed from the center aisle.* ABOVE: *Detail of eight-pointed star in the sanctuary.*

B'NAI ISRAEL SYNAGOGUE | BALTIMORE, MD

HENRY BERGE

BUILT 1875

The synagogue now known as B'nai Israel was built by a group of Jews that had seceded from the Baltimore Hebrew Synagogue (*page 104*) in 1873, during a dynamic period in the history of the city's Jewry. Refusing to accept the 'reformed' innovations being introduced by the Baltimore Hebrew congregation, they formed their own congregation, calling themselves Chizuk Amuno, or 'Keepers of the Faith.' Two years later, the congregation built its own synagogue on Lloyd Street—just a few yards down the street from the Baltimore Hebrew Synagogue.

Chizuk Amuno's stay on Lloyd Street was short-lived. As was the trend across the country, German Jews often relocated to prominent neighborhoods further from the city center as they became more established, while Polish and Russian Jews arrived in urban neighborhoods to take their place. Two decades later, most of Chizuk Amuno's membership had moved to other parts of the city, and the congregation sold the synagogue to the new B'nai Israel Congregation, comprised primarily of Russian immigrants. The synagogue, which soon became known as the 'Russian Synagogue,' is today the oldest continually operating Orthodox synagogue in Maryland.

OPPOSITE: *Entry façade divided by horizontal bands displaying three different architectural styles.*
ABOVE: *Ark with elegant curves and radiant lights expressing one of the finest examples of Moorish-style architecture in America.*

The architecture of B'nai Israel is an eclectic blend of Gothic, Romanesque, and Moorish elements. Each of the three horizontal bands of window treatments in the three-layered façade features a distinct historical style, although the styles are successfully blended to create a single, cohesive image. The building's design contrasts sharply with the Classical style of the Baltimore Hebrew Synagogue, which its original founders had left. Details such as the horseshoe arches that frame the synagogue's three entrances point to American Jews' developing taste for a uniquely Jewish architecture, featuring more exotic vocabularies than were the norm. Inside, the sanctuary features a stunning hand-carved, Moorish-style ark that sparkles with gold-colored trim.

When George Washington was elected President, he wrote to Congregation Mikve Israel: 'May the same wonder-working deity, who long since delivered the Hebrews from the Egyptian oppressors, planted them in the promised land, whose providential agency has lately been conspicuous in establishing these United States as an independent nation...make the inhabitants of every denomination partake in the temporary and spiritual blessings of that people, whose god is Jehovah.'

CONGREGATION MIKVE ISRAEL | SAVANNAH, GA

HENRY G. HARRISON

BUILT 1878

Mikve Israel is the purest example of an American synagogue built in the Neo-Gothic style. Given its ecclesiastic associations, Gothic architecture was less common for American synagogues than other revivalist styles. Still, it did become somewhat fashionable, and several Gothic synagogues did appear around the middle of the nineteenth century in New York and on the West Coast. It is easy to understand why Mikve Israel would build a Gothic synagogue: Henry G. Harrison, the congregation's architect, was known for his churches and had designed a number of Neo-Gothic buildings. In addition, at the time of Mikve Israel's construction, a Neo-Gothic Presbyterian church stood not more than 60 feet away on the very same square in Savannah.

The third-oldest congregation in the United States, Mikve Israel was established by Sephardic Jews just five months after the State of Georgia was founded in 1733. Although it may not seem quintessentially Jewish in character, the synagogue is a good copy of the type of Gothic architecture prevalent in Europe in the fourteenth century. Gothic motifs include pointed arches over the entries, stained glass windows with tracery, pinnacles that rise above the façade, buttresses, and a two-stage tower. The floor plan is a typical Latin cross. There is, however, one interesting deviation from the standard Gothic vocabulary. Instead of the customary steeple, the synagogue's tower culminates in an anomalous Islamic cupola—a Middle Eastern element hinting at the true Jewish nature of the building.

OPPOSITE: *Entry tower crowned with an Islamic cupola that contrasts with the building's Gothic architecture.*
ABOVE: *Sanctuary in the Gothic Revival style.*

ELDRIDGE STREET SYNAGOGUE | NEW YORK, NY

PETER AND FRANCIS WILLIAM HERTER

BUILT 1887

In 1887, New York City's Lower East Side—the most densely populated place in the world at that time—was home to some 300,000 Jewish immigrants. Although there were countless small, one-room shuls, or shtieblach, in the neighborhood, the Eldridge Street synagogue, built that year by members of the K'Hal Adath Jeshuran congregation, was the first freestanding synagogue built by Eastern European Jews in America. Located in the heart of an area characterized as much by its poverty as by its vibrancy, this imposing building was a symbol of Eastern European Jews' cultural and economic triumphs. The legacy of these early immigrants has been long lasting: today, some 80 percent of American Jews can claim Eastern European ancestry.

Older congregations had constructed a few synagogues—such as B'nai Jeshuran on Greene Street and Anshe Chesed on Norfolk Street—on the Lower East Side, but the German Jewish immigrants who built them had moved to wealthier neighborhoods uptown by the time that Eldridge Street was built. Some of these established Jews became the bosses of the new immigrants who worked in the garment factories scattered throughout the Lower East Side.

The acculturated German Jews and the new Eastern European immigrants had contrasting religious sensibilities, as well as cultural and economic differences. When they moved uptown, the German Jews primarily built Reform synagogues with immense façades, dignified interiors, and family pews. The construction of the Eldridge Street Synagogue signaled—to non-Jews, and to the German Jews who were embarrassed by the poverty and 'Old World' manner of the new immigrants—that Eastern European Jews, like their predecessors, could also thrive in America.

OPPOSITE: *View of entry façade from above.*
ABOVE: *Entry façade along Eldridge Street.*

The architecture of the building is a lively, eclectic blend of the Moorish, Romanesque, and Gothic Revival styles. Islamic motifs, such as horseshoe arches and masonry detailing, are juxtaposed with a Gothic rose window that dominates the central façade. The combination of Eastern and Western vocabularies distinguishes the synagogue from contemporary churches, but it fits within the larger context of historic revivalism that was popular in America at the time. Though no longer in regular use today, the synagogue is maintained by the Eldridge Street Project, a non-profit organization that offers programs in and tours of the building, which it is faithfully restoring to its original condition.

LEFT: *The sanctuary, currently unrestored.*
ABOVE: *View of parapet detailing with the Williamsburg Bridge.*

GEMILUTH CHASSED | PORT GIBSON, MS

BARTLETT & BUDEMEYER

BUILT 1892

Gemiluth Chassed, the oldest synagogue in Mississippi, stands out as an exotic building even in Port Gibson, the town that Ulysses S. Grant, during the Civil War, declared 'too beautiful to burn.' German Jews had first settled in Port Gibson—and a number of other southern towns—during the middle of the nineteenth century. They had arrived as itinerant peddlers, but eventually became part of the town's merchant class.

Although they quickly organized a congregation, Port Gibson's Jews did not build a synagogue until the 1890s, following the influx of Eastern European immigrants. At that time, Eastern architectural motifs were still a popular choice for synagogues, as evidenced by the eclectic mix of Moorish and Byzantine elements used here. At Gemiluth Chassed, the bulbous, pointed dome recalls the type of onion domes that were common in medieval Russian structures, and in the Byzantine-style buildings built in Germany and the Balkans during the Ottoman period. By the end of the nineteenth century, countless synagogues with bulbous domes had been built by Jewish groups across the country. These vernacular buildings—like Gemiluth Chassed—generally appeared in smaller towns and rural areas, and contrasted sharply with the majestic Moorish synagogues built decades earlier by more established Jewish congregations.

Sadly, Gemiluth Chassed has not been used since 1974, since by that time most of Port Gibson's Jews had moved on to major cities such as New Orleans, Jackson, and Memphis. The fact that it still stands at all is a rather incredible tale of preservation. In 1986, the building was saved from the wrecking ball when a local family decided to purchase it. Today, it is completely renovated, and it stands as one of the last remnants of the town's once prosperous Jewish community. The synagogue is now open to Jewish groups and the general public for building tours and events.

OPPOSITE: *Façade with the large bulbous-pointed domes that dominate the small-scale building.*

ABOVE: *Ark tucked inside a decorative, semicircular apse.*

TEMPLE B'NAI SHALOM | BROOKHAVEN, MS

ARCHITECT UNKNOWN

BUILT 1896

Temple B'nai Shalom is a quaint vernacular building located an hour south of Jackson in Brookhaven, Mississippi. Its façade features an eclectic array of decorative motifs, none of which make overt reference to the Jewish nature of the building.

Jews settled in Brookhaven in the 1890s and soon established themselves as merchants and traders. Seeds for the building of their synagogue were planted when five women, members of the local Ladies Hebrew Society, organized to construct a house of worship. They wrote to several Brookhaven firms that did business with their husbands, asking for funds to build a synagogue, and in 1896 the building was constructed. Although the congregation never hired a full-time rabbi, visiting rabbis from Nashville, Hattiesburg, Natchez, McComb, Vicksburg, and New Orleans all lent their support. After World War II, Brookhaven's Jewish population began to decline, and by the 1970s the synagogue offered services only on the High Holidays.

On the exterior of Temple B'nai Shalom, subtle Eastern motifs such as the horseshoe-shaped entryway and windows are juxtaposed with more traditional American elements such as the scallop cladding in the pediment. The tower at the building's entrance is quietly ornamented with a fleur-de-lis pattern at its top, while a slender window below references the porthole of an Islamic minaret. Inside the building, the sanctuary is refined and simple, and is almost entirely white except for the stained glass ornamenting the windows. The modest, cabinet-style ark is set into a niche directly behind the lecterns and chairs at the bimah, which are thought to date back to the founding of the congregation.

OPPOSITE: *Simple and unadorned sanctuary evokes a serene intimacy.*
ABOVE: *Entry façade with its short, broad tower.*

CONGREGATION AHAVATH BETH ISRAEL

BOISE, ID

CHESTNEY AND SCHROEDER

BUILT 1896

The Ahavath Beth Israel Synagogue is a tribute to the persistence of the small Jewish community that has flourished in Boise since the nineteenth century, managing to keep its spiritual faith intact without the resources and support services that Jews living in large American cities enjoyed. Jews first arrived in Boise during the gold mining boom of the 1860s, and they quickly established themselves in small businesses. Initially they prayed in each other's homes, and in 1885 they organized a Reform congregation, Congregation Beth Israel. They used a converted space until 1896, when they built the current synagogue, which today serves Boise's entire Jewish community.

The building is composed of a local sandstone base, with a below-grade social hall and a shingle-clad sanctuary on the second floor. The shingles were originally painted red to emulate bricks. Although the architects described the style as modern Moorish when it was built, the synagogue actually integrates Gothic features with Northwestern elements such as locally-quarried stone and overhanging roofs.

Decades after the synagogue's construction, Eastern European Jews came to Boise and formed an Orthodox congregation, Ahavath Israel. In the 1980s, the two congregations merged and eventually hired their first rabbi. Today, the synagogue is used for Reform services on Friday nights, and more traditional services on Saturday mornings. The congregation currently plans to build a new religious complex at another site, and to transport this historic synagogue to the new location.

OPPOSITE: *View of façade at night, emphasizing the synagogue's mixture of exotic architectural styles executed in local materials.* ABOVE: *View of the sanctuary from the bimah.*

CONGREGATION SHEARITH ISRAEL
(SPANISH & PORTUGUESE SYNAGOGUE)
NEW YORK, NY

ARNOLD BRUNNER

BUILT 1897

OPPOSITE: *View from the women's gallery of the bimah and open central aisle plan of the Sephardic tradition.*

ABOVE: *Daily chapel affectionately called 'the little synagogue' with contents relocated from the congregation's original Mill Street Building.*

Three-and-a-half centuries ago, the first Jewish settlers in America founded Congregation Shearith Israel. Eighty years later, that congregation built the Mill Street Synagogue, the first synagogue ever constructed in the United States. Today, Shearith Israel makes its home on Central Park West in Manhattan, the congregation's fifth house of worship in New York. The synagogue—an architecturally significant building designed by a well-known American Jew—is the culmination of an impressive lineage.

The founders of Shearith Israel were Spanish and Portuguese Jews, who arrived in New Amsterdam in 1654. They had emigrated from Recife, Brazil, where the Portuguese had recently defeated the Dutch and taken control of the city. Fearing the harsh consequences of the Catholic Inquisition, the Jewish community fled. Some returned to Amsterdam (where many families had lived since leaving Spain in 1492), while others moved to places such as St. Thomas, Jamaica, Surinam, and Curaçao in the Caribbean, where they founded new congregations. Twenty-three of the refugees made up the group that went to New Amsterdam.

Until 1824, Shearith Israel was the only Jewish congregation in New York, and it was the center of Jewish life in the city. All New York Jews belonged to Shearith Israel, whether they were Sephardic or Ashkenazic, Portuguese or German, because it was the only institution that provided for their religious, educational, and social needs. Later, when Jews from Central Europe began arriving in significant numbers, they formed their own congregations. Over the years, even as other American Jews introduced progressive reforms into Jewish religious practice, the members of Shearith Israel have

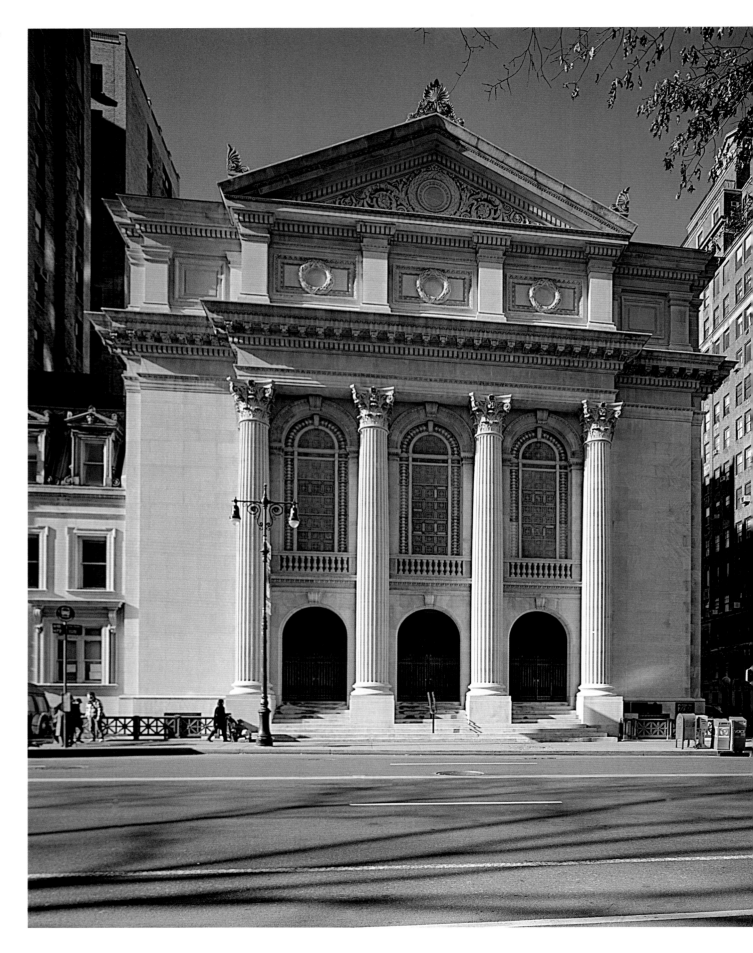

always maintained the Sephardic minhag (tradition). They continue to do so today, and Jews of both Sephardic and Ashkenazic heritage still pray there.

Over the course of its history, Shearith Israel has built synagogues in four separate locations in New York. The congregation built its first synagogue on Mill Street (now South William Street) in Lower Manhattan in 1730. As its membership became more successful, the congregation moved north, building new synagogues in 1831 and 1860 at locations progressively further uptown. In the 1890s, the congregation purchased several lots on Central Park West, and hired noted architect Arnold Brunner to design its current building. The first American-born Jewish architect, Brunner became a proponent of Neo-Classical design during a time when the Moorish style was still popular for synagogues. Brunner had built synagogues with Oriental elements earlier in his career, but by the time he was hired by Shearith Israel he was arguing that the Moorish style was little more than a passing fad, with little historic relevance. Brunner pointed to recent excavations in Palestine of ancient synagogues strongly influenced by Roman architecture. He went on to design a number of Neo-Classical synagogues in New York, of which Shearith Israel is the most renowned.

Facing Central Park, Shearith Israel's eastern and most public façade features three large Tiffany stained-glass arch windows, framed by four tall, majestic columns. Despite the placement of these three grand entranceways, this façade is basically a faux entrance, as the opening here leads only to two small, seldom-used side doors.

OPPOSITE: *Classical Revival entry façade along Central Park West.*
ABOVE: *Sanctuary with its open central aisle seating plan.*

The primary entrance to the building is in fact on the north side of the building—Brunner could not place the main entrance on the eastern side of the building because the congregation had insisted that the ark be placed along the eastern wall, following Jewish tradition. But the congregation must have also felt it was essential to have a commanding presence on prestigious Central Park West, and endorsed the building of a grandiose—albeit deceptive—façade.

Inside the sanctuary, almost every detail has a serene and elegant quality. Smooth marble was used for the ark and the wall that surrounds it, and oil-burning lights surround the bimah. Plush velvet benches are placed according to the traditional Sephardic layout, an arrangement that the congregation has used in all of its synagogues. From the north and south walls, the men's seating slopes down to the center of the sanctuary, while the women's gallery wraps around the room on three sides. Tiffany glass panels located behind the women's section change hues according to the light that filters in from outside. These windows, along with almost every element of the synagogue, were restored in a major renovation project completed in 2003.

OPPOSITE: Ner tamid *(eternal light) in the main sanctuary.*

OHEF SHOLOM | NORFOLK, VA

FERGUSON, CALROW & WREN ARCHITECTS

BUILT 1918

Jews have lived in Virginia since 1791, just two years after the signing of the Constitution. In 1844, a small group of German Jews living in Norfolk established House of Jacob, the first congregation in the state. In the decades that followed, more and more Jewish immigrants arrived in search of economic opportunities, and gradually became established members of Norfolk society. During the Civil War, many members from House of Jacob served in the 6th Virginia Regiment of the Confederacy. But for much of the nineteenth century, Virginia's Jews were barred from entering public institutions such as hospitals, universities, government, and social clubs. As a result, the synagogue served as the center of Jewish life including many social and religious activities.

In 1869, as the congregation's members continued to assimilate, it changed its name to Ohef Sholom, or 'Lovers of Peace.' Ideological differences between members of the congregation came to a head when more liberal members of the congregation proposed a series of liturgical reforms, which were put to a vote and swiftly passed. As a result, in 1870, the more traditional members left the congregation. The remaining congregants at Ohef Sholom rapidly adopted the proposed changes, and the donning of kippot, the use of Hebrew, the koshering of meats, and other traditional rituals were discarded. In 1902, the congregation built a Baroque synagogue, considered one of the most handsome religious structures in the South. The building was used until 1916, when a fire gutted its interior, destroying everything but the Torah scrolls. The congregation found a new location, and set about constructing its present building. In general, its architecture reflects the Neo-Classical Revival that was popular at the

OPPOSITE: *Ark and bimah in the main sanctuary. The Torah scrolls are visible behind a metal grille.*
ABOVE: *Classic Revival entry portico.*

beginning of the twentieth century; interior details and decoration, such as the Stars of David on either side of the eastern wall, provide slight visual clues to the building's function as a Jewish house of worship. The sanctuary provides a wide, expansive place for prayer, and light streams in through high, large windows on each side. A raised stage in the front of the sanctuary provides space for the ark and bimah.

LEFT: *Main sanctuary with seating removed.*

VILNA SHUL | BOSTON, MA

MAX KALMAN

BUILT 1920

Located in Beacon Hill, Vilna Shul was built by Lithuanian Jews who immigrated to Boston at the turn of the nineteenth century. Its founders were part of the massive influx of Eastern European Jews who immigrated to America at the turn of the nineteenth century and settled in cities throughout the Northeast. In 1893, a group of Jews from Vilna, Lithuania formed a *landsmanshaft*, an informal place for worship and community events for Jews who had emigrated from the same city or town in Europe. This *landsmanshaft* later became the Vilna Congregation, an Orthodox shul, and in 1920, the congregation constructed its small but lovely synagogue.

Though the congregation's members remained in the city long after other, more affluent Jews left for the suburbs, over the years Vilna Shul's congregation dwindled and finally dispersed. The original congregation's last religious service was held in the synagogue in 1985.

The synagogue, which is set back from the street, has one of the few open courtyards along the street in Beacon Hill. Its front entrance leads into a multipurpose room that was originally used for meetings and daily minyans. The main sanctuary is located on the second floor, and its seating areas forms an L-shape that wraps around the ark and bimah. Because the congregation was Orthodox, the sanctuary includes a separate women's section, placed next to the central space on the bimah's right. The bimah is illuminated by a skylight, a relatively uncommon feature in American synagogues that adds a beautiful touch. Like many wooden arks found in Eastern Europe, the ark here is elaborately carved, with a representation of the Ten Commandments' tablets included in the decoration.

OPPOSITE: *The bimah, softly illuminated by a skylight above.*
ABOVE: *Stained-glass window above the main entry.*
FOLLOWING PAGES: *The bimah as seen from southern side of the sanctuary.*

OPPOSITE: *Entry court enclosed by stone piers and iron fencing.*
ABOVE: *The raised bimah.*

In 1990, the building became home to the Vilna Center for Jewish Heritage, an organization that was established primarily to save the rapidly decaying building. During the restoration process, elaborate wall paintings were uncovered beneath layers of paint and painted pilasters were found in the men's and women's seating areas. The pilasters, which recall Greco-Roman forms, may reference the original Temple in Jerusalem. These ornamental images also evoke the vivid polychrome painting of earlier Polish and Russian synagogues.

The Vilna Center has been renamed the Boston Center for Jewish Heritage and today offers various programs, including monthly religious services. The Center hopes to preserve a remnant of Boston's Jewish history by converting the building into the city's first Jewish museum, which will offer Jewish learning programs and exhibits, along with tours of the original shul.

TEMPLE EMANU-EL | SAN FRANCISCO, CA

ARTHUR BROWN, JR., JOHN BAKEWELL, AND SYLVAIN SCHNAITTACHER

BUILT 1926

With its iconic dome that rises above the urban landscape of San Francisco, Temple Emanu-El attests to the ongoing growth and success of a congregation whose roots date back to the earliest days of that city's history.

Like many other California settlers, San Francisco's first Jews came as gold miners and merchants in the mid-nineteenth century, making San Francisco one of the few cities in America that Jews actually helped to found. Jews sought the same opportunities that lured people of every background to the West Coast.

Temple Emanu-El's congregation erected its first synagogue in 1854, when a number of religious buildings were being built in San Francisco. These houses of worship were thought to provide constancy in a city with a reputation for rampant lawlessness. That first synagogue, a freestanding Neo-Gothic building, did little to distinguish the city's young Jewish community from its non-Jewish population. The congregation's second synagogue, built in 1866, was a far more sumptuous structure, designed in the Moorish Revival style, and it was revered for the golden globes that topped the two towers protruding from the synagogue's primary façade. Inaugurating the Moorish style in the city, the globes were one of the most noteworthy architectural features of the San Francisco landscape at that time.

The current synagogue is dominated by its massive, majestic central dome, the most prominent element of a style that the architects called 'Levantine,' referring to the early Mediterranean region, or Levant, where Jews had settled in antiquity. In actuality, the synagogue's design aesthetic—which includes elements more commonly referred to as Byzantine—is only partially influenced by the architecture of the

OPPOSITE: *The grand stair leading to the raised ark and bimah.*
ABOVE: *Exterior with the central dome clad in terra-cotta tiles.*

Mediterranean region. Mission-style detailing and materials pervade both the façade and the interior, the Spanish-influenced elements giving the synagogue a distinctly Californian flavor. Art Deco-type ornamentation is also found in the courtyard and interior spaces.

The synagogue's sanctuary has a square layout, unlike the more typical oblong plan used in many American synagogues. The seating plan is a theater-style arrangement with the ark and bimah located at one end. Because the sanctuary is wider than most synagogues of the time, it accommodates more seats along the sides that are closer to the ark and bimah, the focal points of the service.

Fine architectural details and Jewish art are employed throughout the building. The bejeweled ark glimmers, while the bimah is covered by a stone canopy, supported by four green marble columns.

Emanu-El's design is also an early example of the movement in American synagogue design toward synagogues that could fulfill a variety of functions, serving as community centers. Rabbi Meyer, the Temple's rabbi at the time of its construction, had argued that 'any church or synagogue deaf to the possibility of social and community service is doomed...one thing is certain, that just a house-of-prayer idea for weekly services and religious school instruction is apt to be barren.' Originally, Temple Emanu-El's courtyard led to classrooms, a library, a chapel, a gymnasium, and an art gallery. The gym was converted into a social hall in the 1950s to accommodate the changing needs of the congregation.

LEFT: *The sanctuary.*

ABOVE: *Hand-crafted gates.*

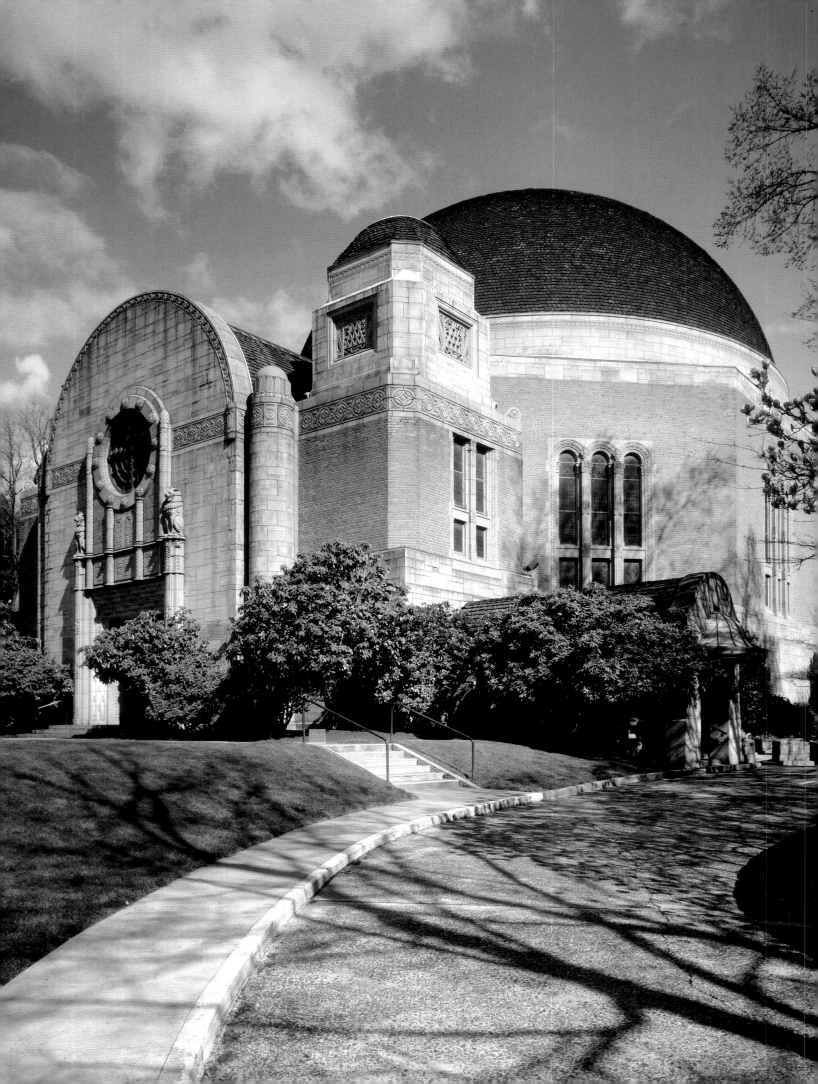

TEMPLE BETH ISRAEL | PORTLAND, OR

MORRIS H. WHITEHOUSE, HERMAN BROOKMAN, AND HARRY A. HERZOG

BUILT 1928

Constructed at the pinnacle of the 1920s economic boom, Temple Beth Israel is one of the greatest examples of Byzantine Revival architecture on the West Coast. The synagogue—the congregation's third home—was one of a number of grandiose synagogues built in America at that time, particularly by prominent Reform congregations. These synagogues symbolized the capacity of American Jews to prosper in America.

Members of the Beth Israel congregation had originally come from Germany, Poland, Russia, and other Eastern European countries, as well as from the eastern United States. They had arrived in the earliest days of the city's development, and by the time this building was completed, the congregation enjoyed a close rapport with other local residents, a relationship that was literally etched into the building itself. In honor of the synagogue's inauguration, Portland's Christian community gave the congregation a stained glass window as a gift. Attendees at the Shabbat dedication ceremony included the city's mayor, George Baker, along with a host of other prominent city leaders.

The history of the congregation's synagogues illustrates changing trends in synagogue design and American architecture over a period of decades. Built in 1859, the congregation's first synagogue was a Gothic structure with vernacular elements, a typical American religious building. The congregation's second synagogue, built 30 years later, was an impressive structure designed in the then-popular Moorish style. It was the largest house of worship in Portland until it mysteriously burned down in 1923.

OPPOSITE: *Entry drive leading to the side entrance and stairs leading to the main entry.*

ABOVE: *The main sanctuary and its central dome.*

The current Byzantine Revival synagogue was designed by three well-respected local architects. This type of architecture had been used previously for synagogues on the East Coast, though Beth Israel is really quite distinct from its predecessors. Byzantine Revival style buildings are typically organized around large central domes, creating sumptuous, spacious interiors that enhance spiritual worship. In the dense urban centers of East Coast cities, Byzantine Revival synagogues were usually hemmed in by neighboring structures, and views of their domes were generally obstructed. Beth Israel, on the other hand, was built as a freestanding structure on an open suburban site; its majestic dome—which rises 100 feet above the ground—thus creates a bold, vertical element that dominates worshippers' views as they approach the synagogue. The sandstone and brick façade is smooth and polished, and it has a certain grandeur, elegance, and grace.

Inside, the sanctuary is an airy, light-filled space. An overhanging gallery emphasizes the upward thrust of the dome, while delicate brass light fixtures descend from the ceiling to the floor.

PARK AVENUE SYNAGOGUE | NEW YORK, NY

WALTER SCHNEIDER

BUILT 1928

In 1928, the Park Avenue congregation dedicated its current synagogue, and the building—with its lavish sanctuary and octagonal domed ceiling—became the emblem of this prominent Conservative community.

Founded as Temple Gates of Hope in 1882 by a group of German-speaking Reform Jews, the congregation made its first home in a converted church on East 86th Street, which soon became known as the 86th Street Temple. As the Jewish community in New York experienced various demographic shifts over the next four decades, the congregation merged with a number of congregations, demonstrating how immigrant groups could cooperate to survive and prosper. In 1923, the congregation changed its name to Park Avenue Synagogue, and three years later began construction of the current synagogue on 87th Street. After a final merger, the congregation became affiliated with the Conservative movement.

Flamboyant Moorish ornament had become somewhat outmoded by the time of Park Avenue's construction, as it had been employed extensively in American synagogues for many decades. As a result, the Park Avenue Synagogue is an eclectic mixture of tastes, not really Moorish, but not purely Byzantine. The ark, for example, is framed by a deeply carved, pointed arch instead of a rounded arch, which would have been more in keeping with the synagogue's other Byzantine features, such as the central dome, a hallmark of the popular Byzantine style that saw countless iterations throughout the 1920s. Inside the synagogue, the sanctuary is decorated with elaborate Moorish-style motifs, from Arabesque dadoes to the 'mugarnas' design of the domed ceiling. On the whole, however, the decoration is fairly restrained, and is used more sparingly than in many other Moorish-influenced synagogues.

OPPOSITE: *Sanctuary with its central, stained-glass dome.* ABOVE: *Raised bimah with seating for clergy and synagogue officials.*

CONGREGATION RODEPH SHALOM

PHILADELPHIA, PA

SIMON & SIMON

BUILT 1928

When the oldest Ashkenazi congregation in America, Rodeph Shalom, built its current home in the Byzantine Revival style, the members wanted to demonstrate that they were progressive and modern. The congregation was founded in 1795 by a group of German Jewish immigrants who had left Philadelphia's established Sephardic congregation, Mikveh Israel, due to cultural and liturgical differences. In order to distinguish themselves from the Sephardic congregation, they called themselves the 'German Hebrew Congregation Rodeph Shalom.'

The existing synagogue is the congregation's third home. Rodeph Shalom had originally rented space, but prior to building this synagogue the congregation had built and worshipped in an equally impressive building. Located on the same site where the current synagogue now stands, Rodeph Shalom's second synagogue was a grand Moorish building designed by the prominent Philadelphia firm of Frazer, Furness and Hewitt. When it was built in 1871, various physical characteristics of the new sanctuary indicated that the congregation's values were beginning to change. Women sat on one side of the sanctuary, across from the men, instead of sitting in a separate gallery. Both men's and women's pews faced the ark and bimah, which for the first time was turned to face the congregants instead of the ark. The congregation continued to liberalize, and by 1901 it had broken completely with the strict traditions of Orthodox Judaism.

A few decades later, when the congregation invited Cleveland-based Rabbi Louis Wolsey to become Rodeph Shalom's new rabbi, he agreed to come to Philadelphia on one condition: he wanted the congregation to build a modern synagogue. The

OPPOSITE: *Main sanctuary with the central dome and theater-style seating facing the raised ark and bimah.*
ABOVE: *The triple-arched main entry.*

congregation agreed, demolished their existing building, and constructed the synagogue that stands today. Rabbi Wolsey's demand, along with the congregation's willingness to meet it, indicates that the glorious epoch of the Moorish style was coming to an end. In its place, the congregation opted for a more current—albeit more eclectic—house of worship.

The present synagogue, a large, rectangular Byzantine Revival structure, is simpler than the Frazer, Furness and Hewitt synagogue. The massing is square and the exterior has an Art Deco character interspersed with Islamic references. Inside the building, however, there is the same kind of vivid ornament and detailing featured in Moorish synagogues. The walls at Rodeph Shalom are hand-stenciled, and the tiled floor is brought to life by bright, intermeshing patterns. The ark is built of Italian marble, a popular material for arks at the time; its massive Italian bronze doors weigh 1000 pounds each.

OPPOSITE: *Exuberant mosaic floor of the entry lobby.*
ABOVE: *Ark in the main sanctuary.*

TEMPLE EMANU-EL | NEW YORK, NY

ROBERT D. KOHN, CHARLES BUTLER, AND CLARENCE STEIN

BUILT 1929

Temple Emanu-El is a colossal building that houses one of the world's most prominent Reform congregations. Founded by Western European Jewish immigrants who lived humbly in New York's Lower East Side in the middle of the nineteenth century, the congregation eventually included some of the most prosperous members of New York and national society. In 1929, the congregation proclaimed its success by building an impressive new synagogue—the largest in the world.

Primarily of German origin, the congregation's founding members had first worshipped in second-floor rooms that they rented on the Lower East Side and later, in two different churches that they converted for Jewish services. The Emanu-El congregation was part of the early Reform movement in America, and was one of the first congregations to allow men and women to sit together in the synagogue. By the 1860s, its members became more affluent and moved further uptown, and the congregation began work on its first synagogue building. In September 1868, it dedicated a lavish building on 43rd Street in Manhattan that was designed by two well-known synagogue architects: Henry Fernbach and Leopold Eidlitz, the first known Jewish architect to practice in the U.S. The synagogue, which was hailed as 'the finest example of Moorish architecture in the Western World,' combined a stately composition with Oriental accents, including lacy decoration on the exterior of the building and two minaret-style towers. The building's positive reception helped legitimize the use of Middle Eastern themes and exotic motifs for Jewish American houses of worship.

OPPOSITE: *The main sanctuary, with its impressive scale.*
ABOVE: *Entry façade along Fifth Avenue.*

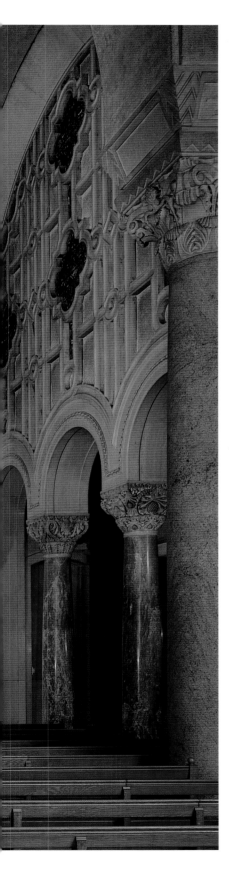

As the congregation grew and prospered, the 2300-seat synagogue on 43rd Street became inadequate. The congregation set about building an even larger synagogue further uptown, at the intersection of Fifth Avenue and 65th Street in New York's most posh residential neighborhood, the Upper East Side. One of New York's most renowned religious landmarks, the current building is a Romanesque marvel with Gothic and church-like references. Its massive main entry portals are its most iconic features. Throughout the 1920s, a number of synagogues, such as Rodeph Sholom (*page 254*), had been built in New York with large arched entrance portals. The entrance at Emanu-El, however, far surpassed those of other local synagogues in its monumental size and grandeur.

LEFT: *Small auxiliary chapel.*

WILSHIRE BOULEVARD TEMPLE | LOS ANGELES, CA

A.W. EDELMAN

BUILT 1929

Wilshire Boulevard Temple broke with tradition in a dramatic way: its sanctuary walls feature paintings with human forms. Typically, Jews have avoided using human forms in synagogue decoration, adhering to a strict reading of the Second Commandment's prohibition of idolatry. By commissioning these murals, the Wilshire Boulevard congregation proclaimed its belief that modern Jews did not have to interpret this commandment literally.

Initially founded in 1862 as Congregation B'nai B'rith, Wilshire Boulevard is the oldest congregation in Los Angeles. Over the years, it has had three homes. In 1863, the congregation built a relatively modest Gothic structure on Fort Street (now Broadway, south of Second Street), and in 1896 it moved to a larger building on Ninth and Hope streets. The current synagogue, which was dedicated in 1929, is a Byzantine Revival building whose exterior composition includes a massive dome, several slender cupolas, and other Eastern decorative motifs.

The murals form an integral part of the sanctuary and infuse the building with a spirit of drama and fantasy. They depict several biblical stories, including some of the most significant moments in Jewish history. Rather than suggesting a literal reading of the histories that they recount, the artworks inspire a sense of warmth and mysticism that was previously lacking in many Reform synagogues across the United States. Apart from their ability to create a more spiritual, contemplative sanctuary, this type of representation was particularly appropriate for its time and place. The film and television industries were becoming dominant in Los Angeles and visual imagery was becoming a more important part of American culture. Hugo Ballin, the artist who

OPPOSITE: *The central, coffered dome of the sanctuary.*
ABOVE: *Exterior.*

painted the murals, had been a prolific film producer and director, returning to painting in the late 1920s after the advent of talking pictures. Furthermore, many significant Hollywood personalities were members of the congregation, including Jack, Harry, and Abe Warner of Warner Brothers, who funded the murals.

The congregation believed that it had made history by incorporating murals with human figures, but just a few years after the completion of the Wilshire Boulevard Temple, archeologists discovered magnificent murals at an ancient synagogue at Dura-Europos, Syria, that was built around 245 A.C.E. With its elaborate images of Jewish heroes and Biblical scenes, the Dura-Europos synagogue debunked a common misconception, providing evidence that even in antiquity Jews had in fact used human imagery, much as the Wilshire Boulevard Temple congregation had done.

LEFT: *The sanctuary with painted murals that wrap around the lower walls and crown the arches.*

THE TEMPLE | ATLANTA, GA

HENTZ, ADLER & SHUTZE

BUILT 1931

The Temple is the oldest Jewish congregation in a city where Jews have lived since 1844. Organized in 1866, The Temple was affiliated with Orthodox Judaism until the late-nineteenth century, when the congregation adopted the practices of the growing Reform Movement. The architecture of The Temple, with its combination of Classical and American vernacular elements, serves as a proud symbol of the Jewish community's long-lasting presence in Atlanta.

Jews, however, have not always been accepted in Atlanta society. During their first years of living in the city, Jews were banned from many professions and social organizations. A member of The Temple's congregation, Leo Frank, is the only white man ever known to have been lynched. Frank, who had been falsely accused of murdering a 14-year-old employee in his pencil factory, was murdered in 1915 by an incensed mob after his sentence was commuted to life imprisonment instead of the death penalty. Years later, Frank was exonerated of the crime.

In the middle of the twentieth century, at the height of the Civil Rights movement, The Temple itself became an object of attack when senior rabbi Jacob Rothschild voiced his commitment to working for the equality of the black and white citizens of Atlanta. In October 1958, members of the Klu Klux Klan blew open the northern side of the building with 50 sticks of dynamite. The Temple was one of dozens of synagogues across the South that were targeted in the late 1950s by anti-Semites, in an attempt to silence some Jews' outspoken views about race.

Atlanta, however, had a reputation for relative tolerance compared to other places in the South, and the attack came as a shock to many congregants.

OPPOSITE: *Ark and bimah in the main sanctuary.*
ABOVE: *Main entry.*

Soon after The Temple was bombed, the synagogue was successfully restored to its original condition with the charity and support of Atlanta citizens of all faiths.

The synagogue is an impressive blend of Classical references and American motifs, such as the red brick exterior and stone detailing. In a proud display of patriotism, the *ner tamid* in the sanctuary hangs from the eagle and stars of the Great Seal of the United States. The ark is gold-leafed and is placed atop a dramatic architectural surround. Its commanding position in the sanctuary, along with the raised reading table, focuses worshippers' attention on the leaders of the service at the front. On both the synagogue's interior and exterior, classical elements are integrated with Jewish symbols and themes; in the sanctuary this imagery—chosen by the congregation's rabbi—is integrated with the plaster detailing.

Today, the congregation is extensively renovating and expanding The Temple, a project that includes the addition of a chapel, the design of which demonstrates the congregation's evolving values. In contrast to the original sanctuary's grandiose altar area, the chapel will feature a more informal ark and bimah arrangement, which is intended to provide smaller, more inclusive services.

LEFT: *The sanctuary as viewed from the balcony.*

ABOVE: *Main entry, after restoration.*

BETH SHOLOM SYNAGOGUE | ELKINS PARK, PA

FRANK LLOYD WRIGHT

BUILT 1954

'We want to build an American synagogue for Jews to worship in,' declared Frank Lloyd Wright when he was commissioned to design a new building for the Beth Sholom Congregation in Elkins Park, Pennsylvania.[1] In choosing Wright—America's most renowned architect—to design their synagogue, members of Beth Sholom articulated a desire to fuse American and Jewish values in a contemporary way, rather than making reference to the architectural styles of the past. When it was completed, Wright had successfully created a synagogue that spoke for American Jews, yet remained unswervingly faithful to his characteristic vision. Congregations across the country were adopting modernist forms, and Wright's Beth Sholom Synagogue—one of the best examples of the trend—demonstrated that modern architecture could fulfill the spiritual needs of Jewish congregations in America.

The Beth Sholom Congregation was established in central Philadelphia at the end of World War I and quickly grew from a few hundred families to several thousand. After World War II, the majority of the membership migrated to the suburbs. Since there were no Jewish institutions in Elkins Park at the time, the recently arrived Jews built a new center that could accommodate a range of functions, including a religious school, a chapel, a large auditorium/gymnasium, a swimming pool, and catering facilities. The highlight of the complex was the sanctuary building designed by Frank Lloyd Wright.

OPPOSITE: *The sanctuary.*
ABOVE: *Pyramid form evokes Mount Sinai.*

Wright fashioned a sculptural body that integrates both architectural modernism and American Judaism. Pyramidal forms of steel, glass, and aluminum soar above a concrete base, creating an abstract form that evokes Mount Sinai, the place where Moses received the Ten Commandments from God. The sanctuary's powerful upward thrust and awe-inspiring expanse are protected by the encompassing structural geometry. The triangular shape of the building recurs in virtually every interior element, including the ark, bimah, *ner tamid*, and even the door handles, imbuing the entire interior with the same reference to Mount Sinai. Thus the sanctuary is filled with Jewish symbolism, without relying on any applied artwork or overt iconography.

Natural light floods the main sanctuary during the day, and after dark it emanates from the sanctuary out into the community. Inside the sanctuary, each congregant enjoys a clear view of the Torah reading and of his or her fellow members. The seating radiates from the protruding bimah like a fan, bringing the community closer together during worship.

1   Frank Lloyd Wright, quoted in *An American Synagogue by Frank Lloyd Wright*, Beth Sholom Synagogue, Elkins Park, PA, 1954, p. 3.

LEFT: *Exterior view of the sanctuary.*
ABOVE: *Abstract stained-glass chandelier.*

TEMPLE BETH EL | PROVIDENCE, RI

PERCIVAL GOODMAN

BUILT 1955

Architect Percival Goodman designed more than 50 synagogues across America. He helped to pioneer a prototype for the modern American synagogue, of which Temple Beth El is one of the earliest examples.

Most of Goodman's synagogues are unpretentious horizontal buildings with a clear organization and structure. They typically feature open, flexible sanctuaries that can change size according to a given event's required seating capacity. Although Goodman was not the only architect to use these design elements, he was certainly the most prolific. He designed or influenced so many synagogue buildings that many American Jews—whether or not they are conscious of Goodman—consider his style to be synonymous with their concept of the modern American synagogue.

Goodman began his first synagogue projects just after World War II, an event that awakened in him a deep sense of belonging to the Jewish community, although he had previously lived a secular life. As a result, many of his synagogue designs emphasize the importance of the synagogue as an all-encompassing community center. For example, Temple Beth El features classrooms, a library, a large ballroom, and a sanctuary that seats as many as 1600 congregants. A large, curved roof covers the sanctuary, and removable draperies along the sides provide expanded seating for the High Holidays and other large services.

OPPOSITE: *Sanctuary lined by curtains at either side that open into additional seating areas.*
ABOVE: *Entry plaza and gardens.*

Although Temple Beth El's context is more urban than many of Goodman's other synagogues, it shares certain characteristics with his suburban buildings. Located in Providence's East Side neighborhood, the unencumbered site allowed Goodman to distribute the synagogue's functions over a large area. As in many of his suburban synagogues, Goodman provided generous indoor and outdoor gathering spaces for both casual activities and formal events.

PRESENTED BY
THE MEN'S CLUB

IN MEMORY OF
ROSE J. JACOBS

IN HONOR OF
THE BAT MITZVAH
OF OUR DAUGHTER
DAFNA ESTHER
MRS. ALFREDO W...

IN MEMO
HARRY F...

CONGREGATION KNESES TIFERETH ISRAEL
PORT CHESTER, NY

PHILIP JOHNSON

BUILT 1956

Constructed for Congregation Kneses Tifereth Israel, this simple, elegant structure was designed by architect Philip Johnson, one of the earliest proponents of modern architecture in the United States. The congregation was established in 1887 in Port Chester, then a small town north of New York City, and first met in the home of one of its founding members. In time, the group was incorporated as Congregation Kneses Israel ('Assembly of Israel'), and built its first synagogue in 1892. As more and more Jewish immigrants arrived in the United States, the congregation continued to grow. Many of the congregation's new members were Jews from Russia and Eastern Europe whose ritual traditions differed from those of the congregation's founders. As they became more numerous, these immigrants splintered off and formed a new group, Congregation Tifereth Israel ('Glory of Israel').

For decades, the congregations prayed in different locations, though they jointly supported a Jewish Center, a Hebrew school, a cemetery and other community functions. Over the years, the differences between the congregations became less important than their shared goals. In 1927, the two congregations reunited and formed Congregation Kneses Tifereth Israel. Although it struggled financially during the Depression and the war years of the 1940s, by the 1950s, fueled by suburbanization, the congregation was ready to build a new home to accommodate its expanded membership.

OPPOSITE: Opened ark surrounded by artwork of sculptor Ibram Lassow.

Johnson's building elegantly juxtaposes two major elements: a domed oval entry and a long rectangular box that houses the social hall and sanctuary. The simplicity of

the exterior forms is echoed by the interior's straightforward design. Colored glass is inserted between the pre-cast concrete blocks of the walls, inflecting the sanctuary with colored specks of light. A skylight illuminates the sanctuary from above. Plaster panels, which are molded into gently curving planes, hang from the building's steel structure. These panels are suggestive of a range of symbolic references, from the tent-like forms of the tabernacle to floating clouds.

In a similar way, the domed oval vestibule suggests a symbolic reference to Israel, located as it is among pine trees imported from Jerusalem. But, as Johnson himself pointed out many years later, the building predates the fascination with symbolic architecture that developed in America over the course of the next decade. Johnson claims that he merely intended to emphasize the play of many colors of light against the pristine white walls and smooth materials of the sanctuary. Here, as in many other religious spaces, the truth of the architecture depends on the meaning that the viewer creates for him or herself.

LEFT: *The sanctuary illuminated by stained-glass windows.*

TEMPLE ISRAEL | NEW ROCHELLE, NY

PERCIVAL GOODMAN

BUILT 1962

Temple Israel is a typical suburban synagogue, built during the period of rapid suburbanization within the American Jewish community that followed World War II. At that time, the majority of Jewish congregations, like many other Americans, began to move out from cities to the suburbs. As they did so, the newly transplanted members required new institutions, and built some 200 synagogues in America during this time.

Founded by a small group of prosperous German families in 1908, the Temple Israel congregation grew during the 1950s when many young families moved into the New Rochelle area. The congregation commissioned Percival Goodman, the country's leading synagogue architect at the time, to design its new building.

Like most of his synagogues, Goodman's Temple Israel embraces its natural surroundings as it wraps around courtyards and outdoor landscaping. It also incorporates the suburban context in that the main approach to the Temple is designed for congregants arriving by car. Whereas earlier urban synagogues usually had bold, monumental entrances on their primary façades, Goodman placed an entry canopy at the top of the driveway where he assumed that most worshippers would enter the building.

The simple, unadorned exterior features Goodman's typical palette of materials: wood, glass, and brick. Inside, the sanctuary is open and expansive. The wooden-beamed ceiling is exposed, and clerestory windows allow the entry of natural light from both sides. Around the time of this synagogue's construction, Jewish artwork emerged as an essential complement to modern synagogues such as Goodman's,

OPPOSITE: *Ark and bimah.*

as Jews began to feel that sculpture, painting, and stained glass could imbue these simple, undecorated spaces with spiritual meaning and could express Jewish identity in a way that would enhance the synagogue's importance in the community. At Temple Israel, Goodman inserted massive stained glass windows that rise above the ark at the back of the sanctuary, as well as dozens of stained glass windows throughout the building that depict Jewish figures and Hebrew text.

Temple Israel demonstrates Goodman's conviction that modern synagogues should serve as multipurpose centers for Jewish communities. In addition to the sanctuary, the synagogue also features a vast social hall for wedding and bar and bat mitzvah celebrations that includes a separate stage for bands. Another one of Goodman's trademarks in evidence here is the movable partition positioned between the sanctuary and the social hall, which allows for expanded seating in the sanctuary on the High Holidays.

ABOVE: *Entry drive with sheltered drop-off area.*
OPPOSITE: *Movable partition connects the social hall with the sanctuary.*

CONGREGATION SHAAREY ZEDEK
SOUTHFIELD, MI

PERCIVAL GOODMAN

BUILT 1963

Congregation Shaarey Zedek is one of the most expressive structures ever designed by Percival Goodman. While many of Goodman's synagogues are horizontally dispersed across their sites, Shaarey Zedek is a conspicuous anomaly; the exterior of the building is distinguished by two pinnacles that jut confidently into the sky. While Goodman went on to design dozens of synagogues after Shaarey Zedek, this building remains one his most assertive projects, embodying Goodman's work at the peak of his career.

Congregation Shaarey Zedek was founded in 1861 when 17 followers of traditional Judaism left the Beth El Society in Detroit to form their own congregation. In the early years of the twentieth century, as Conservative Judaism was gaining momentum in the United States, Shaarey Zedek was one of the movement's pioneering congregations. It became formally affiliated in 1913 when it joined the national organization of Conservative Judaism, the United Synagogues of America.

This is the congregation's sixth building, built after the majority of Shaarey Zedek's members had moved into the Southfield area. The exterior form reads quite differently from a distance than it does from up close, and the reading changes even as congregants approach the synagogue through the large parking lot. An immense, freestanding concrete slab hovers over the entranceway and forms a modernist canopy. From here, the height of the pyramidal form of the sanctuary can be seen looming beyond. The vertical form does not eclipse views of the surrounding landscape, however, because the slope of the roof slants away from the rest of the flat-roofed building. Although the jagged crest of the sanctuary is soaring, it does not overpower the structure, which is primarily horizontal.

OPPOSITE: *The sanctuary.*

As in other contemporary synagogues, Jewish art was integrated into the synagogue's interior spaces. Inside the sanctuary, stained glass windows rise along the edge of the wall behind the ark and bimah, forming a mountain-like crest that alludes to Mt. Sinai. Two movable walls line the spine of the diamond-shaped sanctuary; when they are closed, the sanctuary becomes a long rectangular room with two triangular spaces adjacent to it, one on either side. The side areas function as social halls; one contains a kitchen, and the other is equipped with a stage. The seating is flexible, and on High Holidays, the entire sanctuary and its side wings are opened for congregational seating.

LEFT: *Exterior of the sanctuary.*

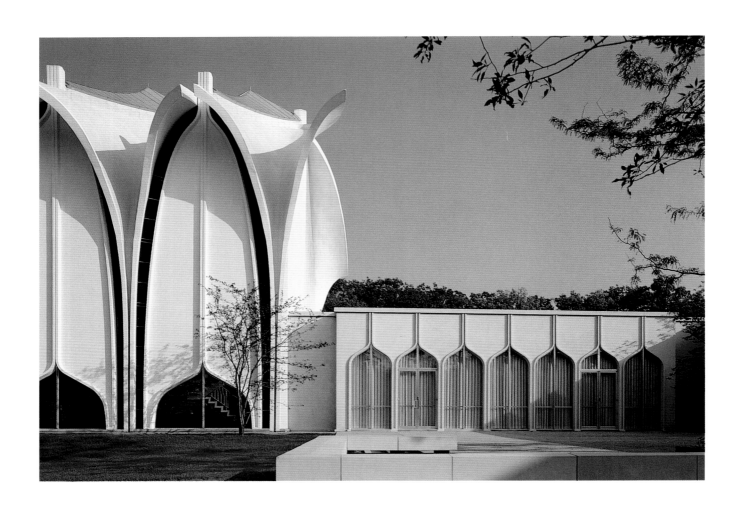

NORTH SHORE CONGREGATION ISRAEL

GLENCOE, IL

MINORU YAMASAKI

BUILT 1964

Finely sculpted and quietly spiritual, the abstract forms of North Shore Congregation Israel evoke a multitude of Jewish symbols with subtlety and grace. The main structure of the sanctuary is composed of arching fan vaults, which might be perceived as hands clasped in prayer, which is not just a Jewish image, or any number of organic forms. Regardless of the way they are interpreted, they imply a sense of the exotic in much the same way that Moorish-style synagogues built a century earlier alluded—in the popular imagination—to Jews' ancient heritage in the Holy Land.

North Shore Congregation Israel represents a period of post-war modernism that was characterized by assertive architectural gestures that had the strength and integrity to stand alone, without applied artwork or Jewish iconography. At North Shore, representational imagery is suppressed in favor of artistic glass and sculptural bravado. The centerpiece of the building is the sanctuary, which is constructed of eight pairs of cast-in-place concrete fan-vault shells that extend from the ground to the peak of the roof. Minoru Yamasaki, best known for his design of New York City's World Trade Center towers (1973), described his sensuously shaped concrete forms at North Shore as a confluence of daylight and solids. The voids between the concrete shells are filled with tinted glass in the upper portions of the sanctuary and clear glass below. The diffusion of natural light and the regularity of the symmetrical elements create a sense of order and tranquility, and the windows provide unobstructed views of the harmonious setting along the shores of Lake Michigan. Inside, details are refined, and functional elements like the ark are fully integrated into the architectural setting.

OPPOSITE: *Exterior, side view.*

ABOVE: *Exterior, front view.*

However, as the congregation learned soon after the synagogue's completion, while the design is very effective when the sanctuary is filled on major holidays, its monumental, 50-foot high expanse can be overpowering for smaller groups and weekly services. To provide a more intimate setting for worship, North Shore, like many other contemporary congregations, finally opted to build a smaller 220-seat chapel. While not as beautiful or architecturally grandiose, the chapel provides a sense of intimacy, warmth, and community that contrasts with the drama and flair of Yamasaki's masterpiece.

LEFT: *The sanctuary facing the ark.*
ABOVE: *The arched windows of the sanctuary.*

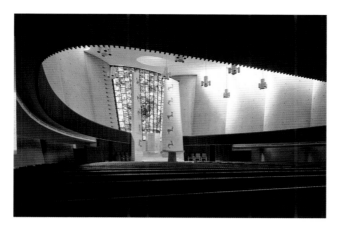

TEMPLE BETH ZION | BUFFALO, NY

HARRISON & ABRAMOVITZ

BUILT 1966

Temple Beth Zion's design reflects a time when congregations across the United States began to hire modern architects willing to abandon the revivalist models of the past in order to convey the Jewish experience in an innovative and artistic way. New forms and materials were seen as ways to bring into existence a new kind of distinctly American synagogue.

The Beth Zion congregation was founded by German Jews in 1850, and by the 1870s, the congregation had shifted from Orthodox to Reform Judaism. The congregation built its first synagogue in 1890, and continued to use it until it was destroyed by fire in 1961. It decided to replace the former synagogue with a more modern design and chose architect Max Abramovitz, best known for his participation in the design of the United Nations Building in New York.

The entire Beth Zion structure acts as a sculptural form. Ten scallops on the exterior, formed by curved pieces of Alabama limestone placed on top of steel-reinforced concrete, represent the Ten Commandments. Bush-hammered walls give the building an aged, mottled effect, thus combining the senses of the old and the new. The walls' outward pitch is intended to resemble a worshipper's arms raised in prayer.

Inside the synagogue, the sanctuary walls sweep around the worshippers in a way that heightens the sense of intimacy. Immense stained glass windows designed by noted artist Ben Shahn terminate the sanctuary at each end. Their panels of blue, yellow, green, and violet compose an abstract mosaic that is segmented by geometric shapes. Lines swirl throughout the entire piece, making a Biblical reference to the

OPPOSITE: *Ark and stained glass by artist Ben Shahn.*
ABOVE: *The sanctuary.*

voice out of the whirlwind that spoke to the suffering Job.[1] Shahn also designed the menorah, as well as the 30-foot-high tablets bearing the Ten Commandments that command the space over the ark. The first Hebrew letter of each Commandment is depicted in mosaic tile, and the text below is written in gold leaf.

1   Job 38: 4–7

LEFT: *Exterior featuring cast-in-place concrete.*

TEMPLE BETH EL | BLOOMFIELD HILLS, MI

MINORU YAMASAKI

BUILT 1974

A marvel of structural engineering, the sanctuary building at Temple Beth El is a modern tabernacle fabricated out of lead-coated copper and cast-in-place concrete. The building soars above the relatively low-lying buildings of the synagogue complex, and is a proud symbol of the 12 German immigrant families who established the congregation nearly 150 years ago.

Founded during the turbulent Civil War years, Temple Beth El is the oldest Jewish congregation in the State of Michigan. Its founding members constituted a significant proportion of the 60 Jews who comprised Detroit's meager Jewish population at the time. Like many other American congregations, Temple Beth El built several synagogues as its needs and membership grew. Prior to leaving for the suburbs, the congregation's last urban synagogue was designed by renowned Detroit architect Albert Kahn in 1922.

When Temple Beth El's membership moved to Bloomfield Hills, modern architect Minoru Yamasaki was commissioned to design its new home in the suburbs. The complete religious complex contains a distinctive sanctuary, a school, a library, a chapel, and a social hall.

The sanctuary is an example of the monumental architecture for which Yamasaki is known, and is reminiscent of the assertive, sculptural modernism employed in his design for the North Shore synagogue in Glencoe, Illinois (*page 192*). Two pairs of massive columns support the sanctuary, which is held together by beams at the top of the structure and at the base. Steel catenary cables are affixed to the beams, propping

OPPOSITE: *The sanctuary with its central skylight.*
ABOVE: *Exterior, front view.*

up the tent-like roof. Inside, skylights crown the pinnacle of the sanctuary and distribute soft, natural light from above. A continuous row of windows provides open views of the densely planted landscape.

In designing the seating arrangements, Yamasaki recognized the need to expand the sanctuary for the High Holidays. Rather than adopting the common practice of expanding the sanctuary into an adjoining social hall, he placed broad, raised platforms around the fixed, central seating. When required, these platforms can accommodate an additional 800 congregants in the main sanctuary, integrating them fully into the inner space of the services.

RIGHT: *Exterior of the sanctuary.*

GATES OF THE GROVE SYNAGOGUE (THE JEWISH CENTER OF THE HAMPTONS) | EAST HAMPTON, NY

NORMAN JAFFE

BUILT 1989

OPPOSITE: The central bimah.
ABOVE: Entry loggia connecting the new building to the original Shingle-style building.

Although the Hamptons—the expansive beaches of eastern Long Island—are best known as the weekend playground of New York City's rich and famous, the area is also home to one of the finest examples of modern synagogue design in America. The congregation was formed in the mid-1950s and its members initially met in one another's homes. As the group grew in size, one of the local churches offered to let the congregation use its building for Friday night services. Eventually, the congregation purchased its own home, an old, local estate that included a large Shingle-style house that was converted for use in services.

For a time, the converted building met the congregation's weekly needs, though on the High Holidays a rented tent was used to seat additional worshippers. Eventually, the building could no longer accommodate the congregation's growing membership and ever-increasing programs, and the congregation engaged Norman Jaffe, a local architect who had made his career designing vacation homes, to build its new sanctuary. Jaffe placed the new building alongside the original building and connected it only at the colonnaded loggia. He designed the new synagogue to mimic the original structure's materials, and borrowed some of its forms, using elements of the popular Shingle style for which the Hamptons are known. In form and content, he created a Jewish house of worship that is unapologetically modern and placidly simple.

The building is composed of a series of fragments of architectural façades, which are tied together with long-span, lightweight trusses. The fragments mimic the profiles of the earliest Hamptons saltbox homes, but together they refer symbolically to the Hebrew letter yad. The space between these solid structural elements is filled with frameless, clear glass that is joined together with clear silicone so that the glass appears to dissolve when natural light enters the sanctuary. The effect is a contemplative space that is surprisingly inviting and intimate, despite its openness to the exterior. In part, the sense of protection is a result of the centrality of the plan, which has fixed pews arranged in a traditional central bimah layout, with the ark in a low alcove behind it. The ark is notably plain and almost unidentifiable, and its sacredness is emphasized not by ornamentation but rather by its special placement in a deep, vaulted pavilion.

The shingles that clad the exterior coordinate nicely with the natural, monochromatic materials of the interior, such as bleached wood, limestone, and sand-colored velvet. Hebrew letters are carved in rustic fashion into some of the wood members, and a few courses of shingles have been formed into discreet Stars of David. While these modest gestures are the only instances of Jewish iconography in the synagogue, the sense of community conjured up by the sanctuary's seating arrangement evokes religious and social feelings in the deepest sense.

AGUDAS ACHIM SYNAGOGUE | SAN ANTONIO, TX

FINEGOLD, ALEXANDER & ASSOCIATES

BUILT 1996

Like many other recently built synagogues, this building represents a bold departure from the congregation's previous synagogue, which had been completed in 1954 and could no longer meet the congregation's needs.

This new home also illustrates the membership's desire to create an architecture that expresses their Jewish identity in a more overt way by recalling elements of the Jewish architecture of antiquity, like Jerusalem's Western Wall.

This approach is becoming more common among American congregations and is contributing to a rise in contemporary designs that incorporate a mix of elements including ancient Jewish motifs, regionalist themes, and Jewish symbols. While the use of varied styles in synagogue design is nothing new, contemporary architects are fusing allusions to ancient Israel with modern architecture in order to establish a connection that is new—that of American synagogues and their connected American congregations—with the Holy Land.

On the one hand, Agudas Achim is a distinctly Texan synagogue building that appropriately reflects a Jewish congregation that was founded in 1889. The exterior walls are enlivened by purples, yellows, and other hues inspired by the local flora of Texas. Open courtyards and windows soak up the 'big sky' light that makes the Texan landscape legendary. Surrounded by a protective wall, the building is entered through heavy cedar doors reminiscent of those typically found in Spanish mission compounds, and the columns that ring the rotunda also have a mission-style feel.

OPPOSITE: *Stone wall in the sanctuary evokes the Wailing Wall in Jerusalem.* ABOVE: *The* ner tamid *designed by Laurie Gross.*

These local influences are blended with subtle references to Middle Eastern architecture, such as the slightly curved windows and archways. Inside the sanctuary, the allusion is far more overt. A great wall composed of stone blocks looms behind the ark and bimah, immediately calling the Western Wall to mind. Moreover, it is fabricated from a type of local limestone whose color and texture perfectly match Jerusalem stone. Several such walls have been built in synagogue sanctuaries across the country.

Synagogues also continue to expand their functions as part of a concerted effort to connect with their communities in lasting, meaningful ways. At Agudas Achim, the 46,500-square-foot complex serves as a community center that includes a social hall, a library, classrooms, and administrative offices.

LEFT: *The entry courtyard.*

CONGREGATION MICAH | NASHVILLE, TN

MICHAEL LANDAU ASSOCIATES

BUILT 1997

For its new synagogue, Congregation Micah opted to integrate symbolism directly into the structure of the building, so that it becomes an indispensable part of the architecture. The center of the sanctuary is dominated by seven steel trusses that rise up and spread into a giant canopy, creating a form that can be interpreted as a menorah or tree of life. The steel trusses are as much a structural element of the sanctuary as they are an aesthetic gesture, because they actually support the roof of the building.

The tree of life that grew in the Garden of Eden has long been adopted as a Jewish symbol, and is particularly rich in associations since it is often used as a metaphor for the Torah, which provides eternal life to all those who study it. At Micah, the steel branches join together over the ark, literally and metaphorically emphasizing the centrality of the Torah in Jewish life.

Solomon's Temple in Jerusalem served as a historical model for the overall organization of the synagogue. The Temple's hierarchical plan was centered on the Holiest of Holies, a private place used by the clergy that was surrounded by a series of public courts. Likewise, the ark and bimah of Congregation Micah's sanctuary comprise the spiritual and physical core of the synagogue, and various community functions are arranged around it: a chapel, a large social hall, a religious school, a library, a computer lab, a new playground, and a gift shop. The cylindrical shape of the sanctuary is the most prominent element, since it stands out from the linear forms of the educational wing and the administrative and support spaces. A playground and sculptural garden for contemplation are also included on the grounds of the site.

OPPOSITE: *The ark, with structural steel, symbolizes a 'Tree of Life' as well as a menorah.*

ABOVE: *The entry façade.*

CONGREGATION B'NAI YISRAEL | ARMONK, NY

LEE H. SKOLNICK ARCHITECTURE + DESIGN

BUILT 1999

This synagogue, completed in 1999, is the first new building for a congregation that once held services in congregants' homes, public libraries, a hotel, and even a converted Lutheran church. A beautiful contemporary house of worship, it bespeaks the surrounding landscape and the quietude which is associated with spiritual study and prayer.

From the outside, the most striking visual feature of the sanctuary is its dramatic vaulted roof which creates a bold identity when seen from afar. The entry sequence toward the sanctuary begins with a low wall that creates a formal procession; its imagery evokes the Wailing Wall while its beige color refers to Jerusalem stone. Extending out from the building to greet congregants as they approach the sanctuary, the wall creates a calming, emotive passageway for worshippers before they enter into the spiritual, interior space.

Inside, the curved ceiling draws congregants from the entrance hall into the sanctuary, where the arch drapes across the grand, airy and light-filled space. Located at one end, the ark and bimah are raised up against a glazed wall that literally brings nature into the act of worship itself. The sanctuary can be extended into an adjacent social hall or the garden where, during the High Holidays, additional seating is placed under a tent. The semi-enclosed garden also provides a distinctive setting for social gatherings, Jewish rituals, and outdoor events.

In addition to these main elements, the religious complex includes a school, administrative offices, a library and a social hall. The library, which is accessed from the main lobby, can also double as an intimate space for smaller events, meetings, and extra classroom space.

OPPOSITE: *Rear façade of the sanctuary at night.*
ABOVE: *Main entry procession along a wall finished to resemble Jerusalem stone.*

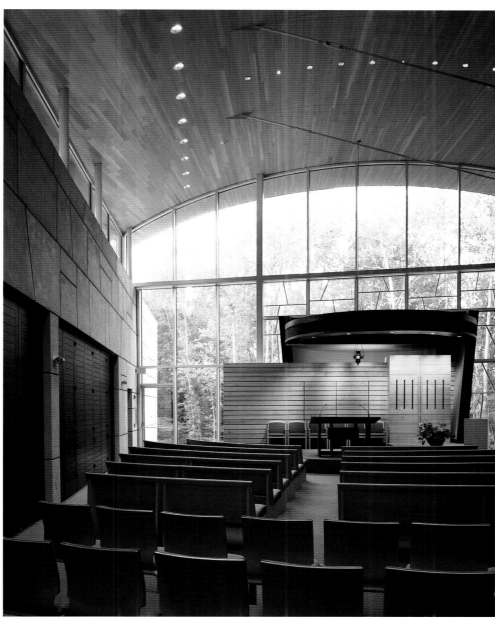

LEFT: *Exterior view of the sanctuary from the side.*
ABOVE: *The sanctuary, with the ark and bimah, as it opens onto its natural surroundings.*

NORTH SHORE HEBREW ACADEMY SYNAGOGUE
KINGS POINT, NY

ALEXANDER GORLIN ARCHITECTS

BUILT 1999

Located on Long Island, this synagogue is home to a young congregation of Orthodox Jews who added their new house of worship onto an existing religious school. The sanctuary's design was greatly influenced by the mystical teachings of the Kabbalah and represents how contemporary congregations are expressing their Jewish identity through interpretive symbolism.

Originally a public school, the academy building was purchased by a local Orthodox community which converted it into the North Shore Hebrew Academy. Building the sanctuary benefited the congregation as well as the school; the congregation paid for the sanctuary and gained its first synagogue, while the school obtained access to the sanctuary for performances and large events.

Newly established, this congregation is open and inclusive in terms of its membership and practice; it is one of the few religious groups in the region that has successfully mixed Ashkenazic and Sephardic Jewish traditions under one roof. The sanctuary's theater-style seating focuses on the reading table and, behind it, a raised platform in front of the ark. A low wall or *mechitzah* divides the seating into two separate sections for men and women, as is customary in Orthodox tradition. Here, the *mechitzah* is designed as a movable partition to make the interior space more flexible.

OPPOSITE: *The raised ark beneath colorful stained glass lights.*
ABOVE: *Stained glass detail.*

OPPOSITE: *Light reflections on the sanctuary walls.*
ABOVE: *The sanctuary.*

Symbolically, the space of the sanctuary evokes the myth of creation according to kabbalistic tradition, which holds that creation came about when the original order of the universe was shattered, an event known as 'the breaking of the vessels.' This shattering action is symbolized by the large aluminum and glass cube that projects up and over the ark. The length, width, and height of the cube measure 20 cubits each, referring to the Holy of Holies which was considered to be the most sacred chamber in Solomon's Temple. At its center are two shifted, inverted triangles which, if viewed from certain angles, evoke the form of a Jewish star.

The intertwined angles of the cube are reflected in the abstract patterns of the *ner tamid* and the stained glass windows that are inserted high into the side walls of the sanctuary and ceiling. These patterns explore the geometric and spatial implications of kabbalistic ideas. As light filters through these windows, it paints the flat, unadorned surfaces of the interior with delicate patterns and richly tinted hues.

TEMPLE BETH SHALOM

HASTINGS-ON-HUDSON, NY

EDWARD MILLS/PERKINS EASTMAN ARCHITECTS

BUILT 1999

Located in a predominantly residential neighborhood, Temple Beth Shalom's new building minimizes disturbance to its setting while maximizing views and natural light. The sanctuary and social hall rest atop the building's base, which is carved into the natural contours of the site, while educational and administrative spaces are located on the lower level. The upper level of the structure is divided into segments of different heights that gently rise above the sloping terrain. Clerestory windows inserted between the segments create a series of 'light catchers,' so-called because they appear to dissolve when they are pierced by natural light during the day. The side walls are also glazed floor-to-ceiling. From the inside, this design has the overall effect of infusing the interior with the landscape around it.

As a result of a limited budget and a desire for simple serenity, the sanctuary and social hall are left largely unadorned. Just as the natural setting pervades other parts of the synagogue, it becomes a source of spiritual inspiration in the sanctuary. Windows overlook leafy trees that were meticulously preserved when the new synagogue was built. Large movable partitions can enclose the sanctuary or expand it into adjacent spaces, depending on the size of the services. The ark is a tall, sculptural, multifaceted form that contains three Torahs. It is permanently installed on the eastern wall of the building. The bimah, on the other hand, can be moved as required when the space of the sanctuary is reconfigured.

OPPOSITE: *The entry façade.*
ABOVE: *Exterior view of the synagogue.*

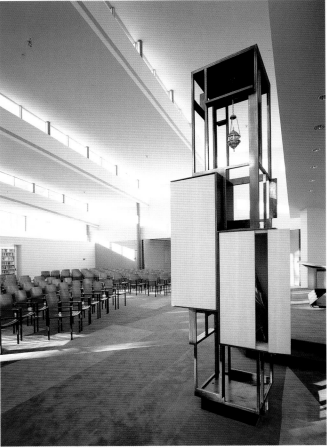

ABOVE: *View of the ark and bimah.*

RIGHT: *View of the sculptural ark and* ner tamid.

FAR RIGHT: *View of the sanctuary from the bimah.*

BETH-EL CONGREGATION | FORT WORTH, TX

HAHNFELD HOFFER STANFORD ARCHITECTS

BUILT 2000

Like Congregation Micah in Nashville, Tennessee (*page 214*) and other contemporary synagogues, this building links its design to Jewish life by incorporating biblical symbolism into its very structure. The organization of the building is partially inspired by Solomon's Temple in Jerusalem, which was laid out as a series of courts leading to the inner sanctum used by the clergy. Beth-El's main entry court is marked by a canopy and an ornamental fence. Beyond the entrance, the landscape is designed as an enfilade of gates and gardens that culminates in the synagogue sanctuary.

The walls of the worship spaces (the sanctuary, the chapel, and the hall of remembrance) are clad in limestone that evokes Jerusalem stone and the Western Wall. Jewish motifs and Hebrew letters are inscribed on the walls and floors. Woven into the rugs are images that refer to ancient synagogues, the walls of the Old City of Jerusalem, and ornate Torah crowns. Elements of the architecture are drawn from biblical sources; two entry columns in front of the sanctuary, for example, represent the pillars of smoke and fire that guided Moses through the desert.

The building includes a library, classrooms, a social hall, and a bride's room, all of which are linked to the Gathering Area, which acts as a central lobby and greeting space for congregants. A lounge-café, open to members of the congregation, staff, and the community, acts as a staging area for Oneg Shabbats, further enhancing life in the synagogue and the congregants' religious worship.

OPPOSITE: *Decorative iron entry gates.*
ABOVE: *Main entry with protective canopy.*

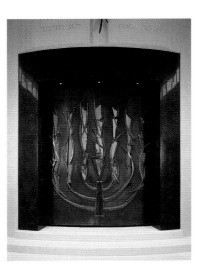

TOP: *Ark doors.*

ABOVE: *The interior entry court.*

RIGHT: *Entrance to the sanctuary flanked by pillars representing the columns of smoke and fire that guided Moses through the desert.*

OPPOSITE: *Exterior, side view.*

TEMPLE DE HIRSCH SINAI | BELLEVUE, WA

WEINSTEIN COPELAND ARCHITECTS

BUILT 2001

Nestled in evergreens, Temple De Hirsch Sinai illustrates how the congregation's spiritual practices have grown more and more intimate over the years. Like many of the grand synagogues built in the late nineteenth and early twentieth centuries, this congregation's first synagogue was a large, imposing, richly decorated structure. By contrast, the airy, light-filled, informal spaces of Temple De Hirsch Sinai's current sanctuary are smaller in scale and more inviting, an example of the less ostentatious worship spaces being created by many American congregations. As in many contemporary synagogues, natural lighting and exterior views are used in place of the colorful artwork and bold iconography of earlier American Jewish architecture.

The congregation's history goes back to the earliest days of Jewish settlement in Seattle. The city's first synagogue was established in 1889 as Ohaveth Sholum, but services ceased there seven years later due to internal disputes over religious practices. The congregation split into two groups, Orthodox and Reform. The former founded the Bikur Cholim Congregation, while the Reform group founded Temple De Hirsch, named after Baron Maurice de Hirsch, a prominent Jewish philanthropist who had helped to fund the passage of thousands of Eastern European Jews to the Americas. In 1971, Temple de Hirsch merged with Temple Sinai, a Reform synagogue in Bellevue, to form Temple De Hirsch Sinai. Today, it has two facilities and a membership of 1450 families, making it the largest Reform congregation in the Pacific Northwest. This new building, which is located just outside Seattle, demonstrates how the local Jewish community continues to grow and evolve.

OPPOSITE: *Glass ark and rear wall of the sanctuary with the natural setting as a backdrop.*
ABOVE: *The entry façade.*

The interior of Temple De Hirsch Sinai creates a sense of serenity and community, and contrasts sharply with the monumental synagogues of the past. Comfortable seating is curled around the bimah in a way that enhances the experience of the congregants as they worship together as a group. More remarkable, however, is the abundant use of glass, representative of a trend in American synagogue design towards maximizing natural light and open views. Behind the bimah and the ark, the entire eastern wall of the sanctuary is almost completely glazed, including one side of the ark. The use of clear glass is a striking departure from older synagogues whose only windows were of stained glass, and purely decorative—their sanctuaries were sealed from outside views so as not to distract worshippers from the act of prayer. At Temple De Hirsch Sinai, the lush landscape creates a spiritual backdrop for the services, encouraging religious contemplation rather than hindering it.

The new building also serves the community's social, educational, and administrative needs. A long corridor serves as the building's spine, linking three pavilions that house classrooms and administrative offices. Each of these pavilions is separated by a tree-filled courtyard, which maximizes the entry of natural light into the wings.

ABOVE: *View of the sanctuary from the balcony.* OPPOSITE: *The exterior courtyard separates the school pavilion from the sanctuary.*

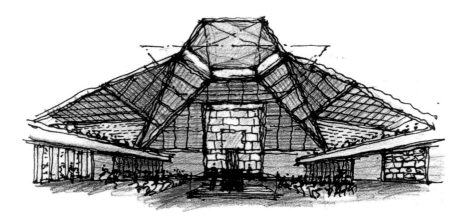

CONGREGATION AGUDAS ACHIM | AUSTIN, TX

LAKE/FLATO ARCHITECTS

BUILT 2001

Congregation Agudas Achim commissioned this new sanctuary with very specific goals for its design: to create a tight-knit space that emphasizes community, and to build a house of worship that reflects the membership's Jewish heritage as well as the Texas context.

The overall composition of the building is inward, complete, and embracing in a way that provides an intimate setting for prayer. The design of the sanctuary itself reflects the tent of the Tabernacle. Four columns form a square and support angled beams, which culminate in two intersecting triangles, forming a Star of David that hovers 40 feet above the main floor. The walls, which stand free from the structural columns, are made of dry, stacked, roughly textured limestone, evoking Jerusalem stone though its origin is proudly Texan.

The plan of the sanctuary has a strong central orientation and highlights the importance of the reading table in the worship service. The seating arrangement also reflects a new kind of organization emerging in American synagogues, in which the seating radiates from a central bimah. In some ways, this might be considered a more 'traditional' arrangement, given that synagogues that predate the Reform movement usually have a central bimah on a separate platform from the ark. However, in this new configuration, the reader's table faces the congregants, whereas in the older synagogues it usually faced the eastern wall, towards Jerusalem. Here, the three-foot-thick eastern-facing wall serves as a backdrop for the simple ark and the eternal light, which hangs next to it.

OPPOSITE: *The sanctuary.*
ABOVE: *Sanctuary perspective by architect David Lake.*

The key source of natural light in the sanctuary at Agudas Achim is a skylight above the ark, which is covered by a tent-like fabric panel. Because there are no exterior windows, the saturated light helps to concentrate the worshippers' attention on the bimah, while making the cream-colored limestone walls appear luminous, creating an experience that has been described as a 'vessel of light.'

Unlike most contemporary suburban synagogues, the sanctuary at Agudas Achim is not expanded for the High Holidays. Instead, a second service is provided in a large, separate social hall.

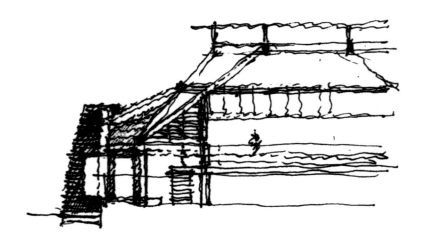

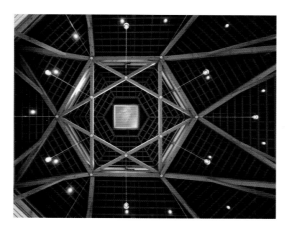

CONGREGATION BETH SHALOM RODEF ZEDEK
CHESTER, CT
STEPHEN LLOYD
BUILT 2001

This Connecticut congregation has created a warm, unassuming synagogue that reinterprets historical forms in an authentically Jewish, yet modern way. Its house of worship was designed to subtly recall the wooden synagogues built between the seventeenth and nineteenth centuries in the *shtetlach*, or Jewish towns, of Eastern Europe.

The early sketches for the synagogue were provided by artist Sol LeWitt, a founder of the artistic movement known as Minimalism and one of most influential artists of the last century. LeWitt, himself a member of the congregation, envisioned a series of tiered wooden forms that were directly inspired by the multi-layered roofs of wooden synagogues in Poland and Russia. Considering that like most American Jews, the majority of the congregation can trace their roots to Eastern Europe, the wooden synagogue was a logical historic symbol to employ, appropriately symbolizing community and inclusiveness while reclaiming Jewish history.

Made almost entirely of wood and glass, the structure sits unobtrusively in its wooded environs, and its interior feels warm and inviting. Immediately within, a large foyer doubles as a lobby area, and provides a place for seasonal art exhibitions. The octagonal sanctuary is quite literally the heart of the building, and it is visible from almost every vantage point inside. Its enclosing walls and bands of clerestory windows provide intimacy while diffusing light throughout the space. The focal point of the sanctuary, however, is the ark, and congregants are immediately drawn to its liveliness. Also designed by LeWitt, the ark is decorated with brilliant colors and interlacing

OPPOSITE: *Skylit sanctuary with circular seating surrounding the modest reading table.*
ABOVE: *Structural beams form a Star of David at the roof's pinnacle.*

shapes that form several Jewish stars, and provides the entire room with an affirming sense of vitality. Above the ark, thick wooden beams form a Star of David within a hexagon; Hebrew quotes are carved into the beams on all sides of the sanctuary. These shapes bring to mind the expressive geometry that characterizes much of LeWitt's work.

The back wall opens out onto a multipurpose room that can be used for social events, meetings, and study groups. It can also be used for expanded seating on the High Holidays. On the other side of the building, a long corridor provides access to classrooms for the Hebrew school and the congregation's administrative offices.

LEFT: *View of the ark designed by Sol Lewitt.*
ABOVE: *Multi-tiered design based on initial sketches by Sol Lewitt who was inspired by the wooden synagogues of Eastern Europe.*

LARCHMONT TEMPLE | LARCHMONT, NY

SCHUMAN & LICHTENSTEIN ARCHITECTS/

PASANELLA + KLEIN STOLZMAN + BERG ARCHITECTS

BUILT 1954/2002

Larchmont Temple exemplifies how many contemporary congregations are seeking more spiritual, intimate places that offer a stronger sense of community and Jewish identity than their synagogues have in the past.

When Larchmont Temple was built in the 1950s, its design imitated the traditional architecture of its locale. The façade of the red brick structure was announced by a simple classical entry portico that was devoid of Jewish symbolism, marked only by a simple English phrase, 'Walk humbly with your God,' which was etched into the stone architrave above the entry doors.

Larchmont's original interior spaces, modern in décor and embellished with contemporary Judaica, were typical of the suburban synagogues of its time. The only traditional liturgical elements in the synagogue were the *yartzeit* plaques adorning the walls, used to commemorate the anniversaries of loved ones' deaths. The sanctuary was designed in theater-style plan, with a stage located at one end of the large room. This stage contained the ark, two podia, and a bimah. A movable partition divided the sanctuary from a social hall, but it also allowed the sanctuary to be expanded as needed.

Recent renovations reflect changes in the liturgy and the congregation's increasingly active role in the services. In the new configuration, the ark and bimah were moved from one end of the room to the center of the sanctuary. In an arrangement that recalls the tradition of placing the ark and bimah amidst the congregation, the seating now surrounds the bimah and the ark, creating a stronger and more intimate dialogue between the clergy and worshippers.

Flexibility is also built into this arrangement: the size of the sanctuary can be adjusted as needed to accommodate varying numbers of congregants. A movable wall

OPPOSITE: *Neo-Classical entry façade.*

ABOVE: *New entry lobby with stained-glass panels.*

LEFT: *Renovated main sanctuary with the movable ark and bimah.*

YOU STAND THIS DAY, ALL OF YOU,
BEFORE THE LORD YOUR GOD.
אתם נצבים היום כלכם לפני יהוה אלהיכם
DEUTERONOMY 29:9

can be positioned to create three different seating plans within the sanctuary, ranging from as few as 100 seats to more than 800 for High Holidays. To maintain a sense of intimacy, the ark and bimah can be repositioned along the eastern wall so that they remain at the center of the service even if the sanctuary is expanded to full capacity. The bimah's design recalls the portability of the Mishkan, the tabernacle the Israelites used in the desert. It is adorned with four poles topped with rams' horns at its corners, as prescribed in the Book of Exodus. The allusion is furthered by the inclusion of patterned plaster panels, which emulate Jerusalem stone and the vaulted ceiling makes reference to the billowing tents of biblical times.

The original stained glass windows and ark door were retained and boldly repositioned in the new plan, while the wall of *yartzeit* plaques has been updated and refined. The traditional bronze plaques with corresponding light bulbs, have been replaced with individual shelves. In a new ceremony, rather than illuminating a light bulb to memorialize the anniversary of a congregant's death, a stone is placed upon a shelf, recalling the Jewish ritual of placing stones upon a person's grave. This new practice is just one example of the way in which individual congregations are redefining the liturgy, reinterpreting traditional practices, and creating their own customs.

Other design elements were employed to enhance the interior environment. The main foyer was redesigned to create a transitional space where congregants can pause before entering the sanctuary. On the wall facing the entry, a quote from Deuteronomy reads, 'You stand this day, all of you, before the Lord your God,' and reminds worshippers of the sanctity of the sanctuary. After services, this area serves as a gathering place for chatting and for greeting family and friends.

OPPOSITE: *View of the sanctuary from the entry lobby.*
ABOVE: *The sanctuary with concentric seating.*

CONGREGATION OR ZARUA | NEW YORK, NY

R.G. ROESCH ARCHITECTURE

BUILT 2002

Or Zarua is a relatively new congregation whose synagogue, like its Jewish practice, is built around notions of community, religious study, and strict egalitarianism. When it was founded in 1989, it was the first new Conservative congregation to be established on Manhattan's Upper East Side in 100 years.

Initially, the congregation held services at the 92nd Street Y and then moved to a nearby church, which it later purchased. As the congregation prospered, its members had to decide whether to replace their existing building or find a larger site where they could build a synagogue big enough to accommodate the number of worshippers that normally attended High Holiday services. Because they were intent on keeping the intimacy and comfort of their small setting, the congregation elected to build a new synagogue on the same property, realizing that they would have to rent larger venues at certain times of the year.

The congregation wanted to emphasize the communal aspect of their religious worship, but the design of the synagogue had to account for the space restrictions of the site. The internal arrangement of the sanctuary is both striking and innovative. Two steeply sloped groups of seats face each other across the central bimah, dramatically heightening the congregation's sense of closeness as they worship together as a group, while accommodating the room's relatively small size.

The sanctuary is largely unadorned, and is without any iconographic imagery. The bimah platform is modest, containing only a reading table, a lectern, and a chair for the congregant who is holding the Torah when it is out of the ark but not being used. An antique *ner tamid* hovers above the east-facing ark, which is flanked by American and Israeli flags, and the composition is completed by a small window that also opens toward the east.

OPPOSITE: *The sanctuary with steeply sloped seating facing the central bimah.* ABOVE: *The eastern-facing ark flanked by Israeli and American flags.*

THE SCHUL | WEST BLOOMFIELD, MI

LUCKENBACH/ZIEGELMAN ARCHITECTS

BUILT 2003

Built in accordance with the traditional Jewish dictate that a synagogue be placed on the highest point of a town or village, The Schul sits on the summit of a 40-acre woodland tract. Members of this Chasidic congregation first came to Detroit in 1958 and immediately began to establish centers in the surrounding areas. The Schul is the first completed building of a complex that will eventually include additional social and educational facilities meant to support the efforts of the Chabad Lubavitch movement to increase Jewish awareness among the area's largely unaffiliated Jews.

The modern architecture of The Schul provides an updated contemporary image for a Jewish sect that was originally founded in the eighteenth century. The structure is 55 feet tall, with impressive windows in the shape of a menorah at each end. The remaining windows are placed at eye level to maximize views of the wooded setting. Inside the sanctuary, the ever-changing tapestry of natural light is The Shul's only decoration. A large eastern window forms the backdrop for a simple ark and *ner tamid* that face a central bimah. Men's and women's seating areas are separated by a low partition or *mechitzah* that can be moved to accommodate different seating arrangements.

The overall environment offers tranquility and invites contemplative introspection. It appropriately evokes the practice of the Baal Shem Tov, the founder of Chasidism, who would retreat to the forest in order to pray in a place surrounded by the wonders of the Creator. The sense of being outdoors is further heightened when the retractable roof is opened for weddings so that they can occur under the sky, as is the Chasidic custom.

OPPOSITE: *Night view of the exterior with an illuminated, menorah-shaped window.* ABOVE: *Removable* mechitzah *in the sanctuary.*

CONGREGATION RODEPH SHOLOM
NEW YORK, NY

CHARLES B. MEYERS/PASANELLA + KLEIN STOLZMAN + BERG ARCHITECTS

BUILT 1930/2003

To complement the services held in its main sanctuary, Congregation Rodeph Sholom recently attached a new chapel, enclosed within a rooftop pavilion atop the historic synagogue. Like many other congregations across the country, the current membership at Rodeph Sholom had become interested in finding ways to involve worshippers more directly in services. They decided to build a new chapel for those occasions when a smaller, more intimate venue could be used.

The fourth-oldest congregation in New York, Rodeph Sholom was founded in 1842 by German immigrants living on the Lower East Side. In 1853, the congregation constructed its first synagogue on Clinton Street, and like other New York congregations, it built new synagogues as its members migrated uptown. Rodeph Sholom built its second synagogue at Lexington Avenue and 63rd Street in 1891, and in 1930 dedicated its current synagogue on West 83rd Street.

The building's façade is an expanse of flat stone, carved with Moorish, Gothic and Byzantine Revival detailing. Inside, the main sanctuary—considered one of the finest religious spaces in New York—has a similar combination of straightforward architecture with decorative touches. The interior is a large rectangular volume with faux stone walls composed of crisp blocks. At the front is an apse that contains the ark and bimah, which are placed on an elevated stage reached by a grand marble staircase; a balcony with extra seating is located at the rear. The congregational choir and organ are concealed behind grille work in the galleries flanking the ark. Considering its size, there are few architectural gestures or details, except for the

OPPOSITE: *The original sanctuary.*
ABOVE: *The new rooftop chapel.*
FOLLOWING PAGES: *The curved wall of the rooftop chapel.*

אשרי יושבי ביתך עוד יהללוך סלה: אשרי העם שככה לו אשרי העם שיהוה אלהיו:
Happy are they that dwell in Your house; they will sing Your praise for ever. Happy the people to whom such blessing flows; happy the people whose God is Adonai.

ceiling and the apse, which are richly ornamented with patterns etched in silver and gold leaf. The space, as a result, is rather austere, a reflection of the formal manner in which its congregation held services at the time when it was built.

In the new rooftop chapel, the mood is still refined, but it is designed to be far more intimate than the main sanctuary. While the main sanctuary has fixed pews that face the ark and bimah, the new chapel has movable seating that surrounds the bimah in an inclusive way. The bimah is not raised, but is set on the same level as the congregants, and as a result, the religious services are more accessible.

Though decidedly modern, the rooftop chapel also has traditional elements that reflect the congregation's return to some of the Jewish customs that its founders had rejected. For example, vessels for storing kippot and tallit have been placed at the entries, because congregants have once again assumed the practice of wearing these ritual items during services. The congregation also made a conscious decision to orient the chapel's ark to the east, as mandated by traditional Jewish law, whereas in the main sanctuary, the ark faces west. As in other contemporary synagogues throughout the country, it features many elements that seek to affirm a sense of Jewish identity. Exterior columns were built with Jerusalem stone shipped from Israel. A long, curving wall acts as a subtle reminder of the Wailing Wall while its scroll-like shape evokes an image of the Torah.

OPPOSITE: *The exterior colonnade of the chapel with columns clad in Jerusalem stone.*
ABOVE: *The ark.*

SELECTED BIBLIOGRAPHY

Architectural Record, *Religious Buildings*, McGraw-Hill, New York, 1979.

Beker, Avi, ed, *Jewish Communities of the World*, Institute of the World Jewish Congress, Jerusalem, 1996.

Benevolo, Leonardo, *History of Modern Architecture*, 2 vols, Trans. by H. J. Landry, The MIT Press, Cambridge, MA, 1971.

Beth Sholom Synagogue, *An American Synagogue by Frank Lloyd Wright*, Beth Sholom Synagogue, Elkins Park, 1954.

Blake, Peter, ed, *An American Synagogue for Today and Tomorrow: A Guide Book to Synagogue Design and Construction*, Union of American Hebrew Congregations, New York, 1954.

Bouchillon, Kim, 'Port Gibson Family to Restore Synagogue,' *Jackson Clarion-Ledger*, 25 November 1986.

Brunner, Arnold William, 'Synagogue Architecture, I–II,' *Brickbuilder* 16, Feb–Mar 1907, pp. 20–5, 37–44.

Cahan, Abraham, 'The Russian Jew in America,' *Atlantic Monthly* 82, July 1898, pp. 263–87.

Castle, Helen, ed, *Modernism and Modernization in Architecture*, Academy Editions, Chichester, West Sussex and New York, 1999.

Chiat, Marilyn Joyce Segal, *America's Religious Architecture: Sacred Places for Every Community*, J. Wiley & Sons, New York, 1997.

Crosbie, Michael J, *Architecture for the Gods*, The Images Publishing Group, Mulgrave, Australia, 1999.

———, *Architecture for the Gods: Book II*, The Images Publishing Group, Mulgrave, Australia, 2002.

Danby, Miles, *Moorish Style*, Phaidon, London, 1995.

de Breffny, Brian, *The Synagogue*, MacMillan Publishing Co., Inc., New York, 1978.

Dean, Andrea Oppenheimer, 'The Beauty of Holiness,' *Architecture* 78, no. 12, December 1989, pp. 68–73.

Dimont, Max I, *The Jews in America: The Roots, History, and Destiny of American Jews*, Simon and Schuster, New York, 1978.

Diner, Hasia R, The Jewish People in America, Vol. 2, *A Time For Gathering: The Second Migration 1820-1880*, The John Hopkins University Press, Baltimore and London, 1992.

Dowling, Elizabeth Meredith, *American classicist : the architecture of Philip Trammell Shutze*, Rizzoli, New York, 1989.

Dunlap, David, 'New Life is Envisioned for Historic Synagogue,' *The New York Times*, 18 February 1987.

———, 'Vestiges of Harlem's Jewish Past,' *The New York Times*, 7 June 2002.

Elman, Kimberly J and Angela Giral, eds, *Percival Goodman: Architect, Planner, Teacher, Painter*, Miriam and Ira D Wallach Art Gallery, Columbia University in the City of New York, 2001.

Emanu-El: Image on the Skyline–Impact on the City, Elizabeth S and Alvin Fine Museum of Congregation Emanu-El, San Fransisco, 27 August 1999–2 January 2000, Exhibition catalogue.

Faces of the Past/Voices of the Future (exhibition), Ohef Sholom Temple, Norfolk, Virginia, 28 August 1994.

Feingold, Henry L, *The Jewish People in America*, Vol. 4, *A Time for Searching: Entering the Mainstream 1920-1945*, The John Hopkins University Press, Baltimore and London, 1992.

Fine, Jo Renee, *The Synagogues of New York's Lower East Side*, Washington Mews Books, New York, 1978.

Finkelstein, Israel and Neil Asher Silberman, *The Bible Unearthed: Archaeology's New Vision of Ancient Israel and the Origin of its Sacred Texts*, Free Press, New York, 2001.

Folberg, Neil, *And I Shall Dwell Among Them: Historical Synagogues of the World*, Aperture Foundation Inc., New York, 1995.

Gertel, Rabbi Elliot, 'In Praise of Percival Goodman,' *Jewish Post and Opinion*, 27 July 1983.

Goldberg, Shari, 'Vernacular Synagogue Architecture,' *Common Bond* 16, no. 2, Winter 2001, pp. 2–4.

Goldberger, Paul, 'Percival Goodman, 85, an Architect of Synagogues,' *The New York Times*, 12 October 1989.

Goldman, Karla, *Beyond the Synagogue Gallery: Finding a Place for Women in American Judaism*, Harvard University Press, Cambridge, MA, 2000.

The Goldring/Woldenberg Institute of Southern Jewish Life, *Cultural Corridors: Discovering Jewish Heritage across the South, Tour III, Alabama to Mississippi, Tour IV, Mississippi to Texas*, Museum of the Southern Jewish Experience, Utica, Mississippi, 2001.

Goodwin, George M, 'My Childhood Temple,' *Faith and Forum* 35, no. 3, 2002, pp. 10–1.

Gruber, Samuel, 'American Synagogue Architecture,' *Common Bond* 11, no. 1, May 1995, pp. 2–3.

———, *Synagogues*, Michael Friedman Publishing Group, Inc., New York, 1999.

Hoffman, Douglas R, 'From Maybeck to Megachurches,' *Architecture Week*, 8 August 2001.

Irwin, Julie, 'Worship's Changing Shape,' *The Cincinnati Enquirer*, 22 October 1999.

Isaacs, Abram S, 'Recent American Synagogue Architecture,' *The American Architect and Building News* 94, no. 1706, 2 September 1908, pp. 74–76.

Isaacs, S.M., 'Of the New Synagogue, Now Building at New York, for the Congregation under the Pastoral Charge of the Rev. S.M. Isaacs,' *The Occident* 4, no. 5, August 1846.

Israelowitz, Oscar, *Synagogues of New York City: A Pictorial Survey in 123 Photographs*, Dover Publications, New York, 1982.

———, *Synagogues of the United States: A Photographic and Architectural Survey*, Israelowitz Pub., Brooklyn, New York, 1992.

Jarrassé, Dominique, *Synagogues: Architecture and Jewish Identity*, Vilo International, Paris, 2001.

Jick, Leon A, *The Americanization of the Synagogue, 1820-1870*, Published for Brandeis University Press by the University Press of New England, Hanover, NH, 1976.

Kampf, Avram, *Contemporary Synagogue Art: Developments in the United States, 1945-1965*, Jewish Publication Society of America, Philadelphia, 1966.

Karp, Abraham, *Haven and Home: A History of Jews in America*, Schocken, New York, 1985.

Kaufman, David, *Shul with a Pool: The 'Synagogue-Center' in American Jewish History*, University Press of New England for Brandeis University Press, Hanover, NH, 1999.

Kennedy, Roger G, *American Churches*, Crossroad, New York, 1982.

Krinsky, Carol Herselle, *The Synagogues of Europe: Architecture, History, Meaning*, Architectural History Foundation, New York; MIT Press, Cambridge, MA, 1985.

Levine, Lee I, ed, *Ancient Synagogues Revealed*, Israel Exploration Society, Jerusalem, 1981.

Meek, H A, *The Synagogue*, Phaidon Press, London, 1995.

Merkel, Jane and Philip Nobel, 'Building for Belief,' *Oculus* 59, no. 6, February 1997, pp. 8–12.

Merkel, Jane, 'Plum Street Temple Study in Symbolism,' *The Cincinnati Enquirer*, 4 September 1977.

Niebuhr, Gustav, 'The Bible, as History, Flunks New Archaeological Tests; Hotly Debated Studies Cast Doubt on Many Familiar Stories,' *The New York Times*, 9 October 2002.

O'Gorman, James F, *The Architecture of Frank Furness*, Philadelphia Museum of Art, Philadelphia, 1973.

Piechotka, Maria and Kazimierz Piechotka, *Wooden Synagogues*, Arkady, Warsaw, 1959.

Pinnel, Patrick, 'Basic Beauty,' *The Hartford Courant*, 17 February 2002.

'Portland, Oregon, Reports Largest Jewish Population Gain in US,' *Jerusalem Post*, 14 August 2000.

Recent American Synagogue Architecture, Jewish Theological Seminary of America and the Jewish Museum, New York, 1963.

Rose, Emanuel, *Temple Beth Israel*, Beyond Words, Hillsboro, OR, 2002.

Sarna, Jonathan, ed, *The American Jewish Experience*, Holmes & Meier, New York, 1986.

Sed-Rajna, Gabrielle, *Jewish Art*, H N Abrams, New York, 1997.

Sorin, Gerald, *The Jewish People in America*, Vol. 3, *A Time for Building: The Third Migration 1880-1920*, The John Hopkins University Press, Baltimore and London, 1992.

Trible, Phylis, 'God's Ghostwriters,' *The New York Times*, 4 February 2001.

Two Hundred Years of Synagogue Architecture, The Rose Art Museum, Brandeis University, Waltham, MA, March 30–May 2, 1976, Exhibition catalogue.

Wheatley, Richard, 'The Jews in New York,' *The Century Magazine* 43, no. 3, January 1892, pp. 323–42.

Wigoder, Geoffrey, *The Story of the Synagogue: A Diaspora Museum Book*, Harper and Row Publishers, San Francisco, 1986.

Witchnitzer, Rachel, *Synagogue Architecture in the United States: History and Interpretation*, Jewish Publication Society of America, Philadelphia, 1955.

———, *The Architecture of the European Synagogue*, Jewish Publication Society of America, Philadelphia, 1964.

Yamasaki, Minoru, *A Life in Architecture*, Weatherhill, New York, 1979.

Zimmer, William, 'Art Takes a Prominent Spot in Chester's New Synagogue,' *The New York Times*, 9 December 2001.

PHOTOGRAPHY CREDITS

6	WEST END SYNAGOGUE, NEW YORK, NY (1996) *Photography: David M. Joseph*
10	NORTH SHORE CONGREGATION ISRAEL, GLENCOE, IL (1964) *Photography: Laszlo Regos*
12	WAILING WALL, JERUSALEM, ISRAEL (2003) *Photography: Susan Herman*
14	SHEARITH ISRAEL, NEW YORK, NY (1897) *Photography: Laszlo Regos*
18	CONGREGATION AGUDAS ACHIM, AUSTIN, TX (2001) *Photography: Hester and Harderway*
20	BIMAH, KRAKOW, POLAND *Photography: Paul Warchol*
22	ANCIENT SYNAGOGUE, KEFAR NAHUM, ISRAEL *Photography: David G. Houser, Corbis Images*
24	SINAGOGA DE SANTA MARIA LA BLANCA, TOLEDO, SPAIN *Photography: Corbis Images*
25 (LEFT)	WOODEN SYNAGOGUE, POLAND *Photography: The Jewish Museum*
25 (RIGHT), 27 (LEFT)	ALTNEUSHUL, PRAGUE *Photography: Corbis Images*
27 (RIGHT)	OHEF SHOLOM SYNAGOGUE, NORFOLK, VA (1918) *Photography: Steve Budman*
30	TOURO SYNAGOGUE, NEWPORT, RI (1793) *Photography: Neil Folberg*
35	SEPHARDIC SYNAGOGUE, AMSTERDAM (1675) *Photography: Suzanne Kaufman*
37	KAHAL KADOSH BETH ELOHIM, CHARLESTON, SC (1794) *Photography courtesy Congregation Kahal Kadosh Beth Elohim*
39	KAHAL KADOSH BETH ELOHIM, CHARLESTON, SC (1794) *Photography: Jacob Radar Marcus Center of American Jewish Archives, Cincinnati, Ohio*
40	B'NAI JESHURAN, NEW YORK, NY (1851) *Photography: American Jewish Historical Society*
42	LLOYD STREET SYNAGOGUE, BALTIMORE, MD (1845) *Photography: Jewish Museum of Maryland*
43	TEMPLE EMANU-EL, NEW YORK, NY (1868) *Photography: American Jewish Historical Society*
44	WOOSTER STREET SYNAGOGUE, NEW YORK, NY (1847) *Photography: American Jewish Historical Society*
47	PLUM STREET TEMPLE, CINCINNATI, OH (1866) *Photography: American Jewish Archives*
48	CENTRAL SYNAGOGUE, NEW YORK, NY (1868) *Photography: Jacob Radar Marcus Center of American Jewish Archives, Cincinnati, Ohio*
56	PARK SYNAGOGUE, CLEVELAND HEIGHTS, OH (1953) *Photography courtesy Park Synagogue*
59	TEMPLE BETH ZION, BUFFALO, NY (1966) *Photography: James Belluardo*
60	KNESES TIFERETH ISRAEL, PORT CHESTER, NY (1956) *Photography: Esto Photographics*
62	GATES OF THE GROVE SYNAGOGUE, EAST HAMPTON, NY (1989) *Photography: Jeff Heatley*
65	CONGREGATION RODEPH SHOLOM, NEW YORK, NY (2004) *Photography: Paul Warchol*
66	TEMPLE BETH SHALOM, HASTINGS-ON-HUDSON, NY (1999) *Photography: Chuck Choi*
70	WEST END SYNAGOGUE (1996) *Photography: David M. Joseph*
71	NORTH SHORE HEBREW ACADEMY, KINGS POINT, NY (1999) *Photography: Peter Aaron/Esto*
96, 98, 99	TOURO SYNAGOGUE, NEWPORT, RI *Photography: Neil Folberg*
97	TOURO SYNAGOGUE, NEWPORT, RI *Photography: Lee Snider*

100	KAHAL KADOSH BETH ELOHIM SYNAGOGUE, CHARLESTON, SC *Photography: Lee Snider*
101, 102, 103	KAHAL KADOSH BETH ELOHIM SYNAGOGUE, CHARLESTON, SC *Photography courtesy Congregation Kahal Kadosh Beth Elohim*
104, 105, 106	LLOYD STREET SYNAGOGUE (BALTIMORE JEWISH CONGREGATION), BALTIMORE, MD *Photography: The Jewish Museum of Maryland*
107	LLOYD STREET SYNAGOGUE (BALTIMORE JEWISH CONGREGATION), BALTIMORE, MD *Photography: Daniel Stolzman*
108, 109, 110, 111	ISAAC M. WISE TEMPLE (PLUM STREET TEMPLE), CINCINNATI, OH *Photography: J. Miles Wolf*
112, 113, 114–115, 116, 117	CENTRAL SYNAGOGUE, NEW YORK, NY *Photography: Peter Aaron/Esto*
118, 119	B'NAI ISRAEL SYNAGOGUE, BALTIMORE, MD *Photography: Jewish Museum of Maryland*
120 (LEFT & RIGHT)	CONGREGATION MIKVE ISRAEL, SAVANNAH, GA *Photography: Lee Snider*
121	CONGREGATION MIKVE ISRAEL, SAVANNAH, GA *Photography: Neil Folberg*
122	ELDRIDGE STREET SYNAGOGUE, NEW YORK, NY *Photography: Bill Aron*
123, 125	ELDRIDGE STREET SYNAGOGUE, NEW YORK, NY *Photography courtesy Eldridge Street Project*
124	ELDRIDGE STREET SYNAGOGUE, NEW YORK, NY *Photography: Roberta Gratz*
126, 127	GEMILUTH CHASSED, PORT GIBSON, MS *Photography: Neil Folberg*
128, 129	TEMPLE B'NAI SHALOM, BROOKHAVEN, MS *Photography: Neil Folberg*
130, 131	CONGREGATION AHAVATH BETH ISRAEL, BOISE, ID *Photography: Andrew Rafkind*
132, 133, 134, 135, 136	CONGREGATION SHEARITH ISRAEL (SPANISH & PORTUGUESE SYNAGOGUE), NEW YORK, NY *Photography: Laszlo Regos*
138, 139, 140–141	OHEF SHOLOM, NORFOLK, VA *Photography: Steve Budman*
142, 143, 144–145, 146, 147	VILNA SHUL, BOSTON, MA *Photography: Samuel Laundon*
148, 150	TEMPLE EMANU-EL, SAN FRANCISCO, CA *Photography: Laszlo Regos*
149, 151	TEMPLE EMANU-EL, SAN FRANCISCO, CA *Photography: Richard Leeds*
152, 153, 154, 155	TEMPLE BETH ISRAEL, PORTLAND, OR *Photography: Michael Mathers*
156, 157	PARK AVENUE SYNAGOGUE, NEW YORK, NY *Photography: Paul Warchol*
158, 159, 160, 161	CONGREGATION RODEPH SHALOM, PHILADELPHIA, PA *Photography: Laszlo Regos*
162, 163, 164	TEMPLE EMANU-EL, NEW YORK, NY *Photography: Malcolm Varon*
166, 167, 168	WILSHIRE BOULEVARD TEMPLE, LOS ANGELES, CA *Photography: Laszlo Regos*
170, 171, 172, 173	THE TEMPLE, ATLANTA, GA *Photography: Timothy Hursley*
174, 175, 176, 177	BETH SHOLOM SYNAGOGUE, ELKINS PARK, PA *Photography: Balthazar Korab*
178, 179	TEMPLE BETH EL, PROVIDENCE, RI *Photography: Laszlo Regos*
180, 182–183	CONGREGATION KNESES TIFERETH ISRAEL, PORT CHESTER, NY *Photography: Laszlo Regos*
184, 186, 187	TEMPLE ISRAEL, NEW ROCHELLE, NY *Photography: Ezra Stoller/Esto*
188, 190–191	CONGREGATION SHAAREY ZEDEK, SOUTHFIELD, MI *Photography: Balthazar Korab*